C000199242

the deeside way

A COMPANION GUIDE

KELLY MORRISON

"Bountiful as she is in greens, Deeside is not a green land... It is predominantly a blue landscape."

Nan Shepherd

WRITING ON *THE COLOURS OF DEESIDE*
IN *WILD GEESE* EDITED BY CHARLOTTE PEACOCK[1]

the deeside way
a companion guide

Words

© Kelly Morrison

Design & Illustrations

© Charlene Cheesman

Photography

© Kelly Morrison

© Elin Beattie

© Charlene Cheesman

Other images credited individually

Printed in the UK

www.kellymorrison.co.uk

CONTENTS

the deeside way

"Knowing another is endless... the thing to be known grows with the knowing."

NAN SHEPHERD
WRITER, POET, AND AUTHOR OF *THE LIVING MOUNTAIN*[2]

It seemed appropriate to start this book by quoting the words of Nan Shepherd. She is someone I have long admired, who had a deep connection to her home on Deeside. Her name and words are woven throughout this book, as are locations connected to her life and writing.

Like Nan, I have lived near the route - which is now the Deeside Way - for most of my life. Some parts I know more than others, such as those walked daily or weekly. It always brings something new, that dual sense of familiarity and wonder. There is always something different to see, a new discovery to make or a new light to view it in, ever changing with the seasons.

I have spent many hours of my life on the path, both on my own and with others. It is a place I seek out in times of both joy and sadness, when I am stressed, when I am seeking beauty and inspiration, or simply to stretch my legs and get some fresh air.

In October 2018 I walked the entire path in a weekend to experience it as a whole - the 'total' route - but it can be explored in many ways. Revisiting it in sections and looking at it afresh to write this book between the summers of 2021 and 2022 has renewed my love for it all over again, which I hope is conveyed through these pages.

The inspiration to write this companion guide came from a friend who had moved to the area and wanted recommendations for his walks, knowing how much I referred to the Deeside Way. It was back when I had my first blog and he had requested a post, but I never quite knew where to start as I had so much to share - from where to get great coffee, to snippets of stories about the history and heritage of the places along the 'Way'.

That was how the idea for the book first started, many years ago, when I dreamed of bringing that all together - to life - on the page. So here I am, offering my suggestions, and sharing my experiences, local insights, and deep fondness for the route, as I would on a stroll with a friend. I am writing about it as a walker, occasional cyclist, and a general meanderer of a place I love. You will also hear from others who love it too.

I hope elements of this book will deepen your understanding, enhance your encounters, and be a companion as you go on your own exploration of the Deeside Way, whether that is in person or from afar.

Deeside & The Deeside Way

Deeside is an ancient and majestic valley which has been much written about since the first tourist guide to the area was produced in 1831.[3]

Fenton Wyness, an artist, architect, antiquarian and author from Aberdeen, who has a plaque at his former home on Salisbury Terrace, wrote in his book of 1968, *Royal Valley - The Story of the Aberdeenshire Dee,*

"The charm of the valley lies in the variety of its scenery. Within a comparatively small area there are great rugged mountains, remote valleys, wild, heather-clad moorlands and lonely lochs, vast pine forests and lush pasture lands. Through it all flows the Dee, twisting and turning on its pebbly course to the sea."[4]

It is an area many people have an affection for - including of course the Royal Family, which gave the valley its regal status of Royal Deeside. As Ivor Brown said in his book *Summer in Scotland,*

"Deeside is called Royal and looks it. It has a sovereign spaciousness."[5]

David Jamieson and W. Stewart Wilson refer to the region in the book *Old Royal Deeside* by *'three R's'; River, Royalty and Relaxation.*[6]

There is also a fourth 'R' which is why the Deeside Way exists now - *Rail.* Many still refer to the track as 'the railway line'...

The Deeside Railway existed for 113 years, closing in 1966. It shaped the landscape, communities and developments that built up along its route. With the railway came the visitors in ever increasing numbers, opening just two years after Balmoral was purchased by the Royal Family, which drew increased attention to the area.

Developed and closed in stages, the railway line's history is fascinating, and many books have been written on the topic, charting its life.

Along the 'Way' there are many opportunities to see remnants of the railway, from embankments and platforms to ironwork, gates and stations, several of which are now private houses.

A taster of the rail journey is available at Milton of Crathes where a mile or so of track has been restored and you can experience journeying by steam train. This was not an original station, but gives a great sense of what that era was like, and it has a range of information and memorabilia from the days of the Deeside Railway.

More on the station can be found on page 86 and at
www.deeside-railway.co.uk

The River Dee (Scottish Gaelic: Uisge Dhè) starts its life at the Wells of Dee near the summit of Braeriach at almost 4000 feet amongst the Grampian Mountains - a focus of much of Nan Shepherd's writing, and described with poetic beauty in her book *The Living Mountain*.

"Here and there in the moss a few white stones have been piled together. I go to them, and water is welling up, strong and copious, pure cold water that flows away in rivulets and drops over the rock. These are the Wells of Dee. This is the river. Water, that strong white stuff, one of the four elemental mysteries, can here be seen at its origins."[7]

It flows a course of over 85 miles before reaching the North Sea in Aberdeen, initially dropping 2000 feet into Glen Dee where it becomes the fastest flowing river in Scotland[8]. It is also one of the most famous salmon rivers in the world.

For stretches of the route, the Dee is not visible, but those glances and sections that it is are incredibly special, and you know it is never too far away.

Alex. McConnochie wrote in 1893, *"On its sparkling waters not a single reach of its scenery lacks beauty or interest, while at many points its charms can hardly be surpassed."*[9]

the deeside way

The Deeside Way is a 41-mile long distance path running from the city of Aberdeen into the Cairngorms National Park and Royal Deeside. The path is suitable for walkers and cyclists with many sections suitable for horses as well. It is Route 195 of the National Cycle Network which is coordinated and promoted by Sustrans.

Whilst very popular with locals, it could be viewed as a bit of a 'hidden gem', being one of the lesser known or publicised long distance trails in Scotland. The path has so much to offer in terms of providing a varied, well signposted, and relatively accessible scenic route.

The path follows the line of the Old Royal Deeside Railway from Aberdeen to Banchory. It then passes through woodland, forest tracks, woodland paths and field margins to Kincardine O'Neil and Dess, and then re-joins the old line from Aboyne to Ballater. This is because the old railway headed north as it left Banchory to Torphins and Lumphanan, before returning to the Dee valley at Dess.

There are plans to maintain, replace and improve signage on the route over the next few years, as well as a programme of surface upgrades. Removing or modifying the access barriers along the route is also intended by Aberdeenshire Council. In terms of gradient and surfacing, the least accessible sections would be through Scolty and Blackhall woods, around Kincardine O'Neil and also Dess.

Notes from deesideway.org:

Most of the route is off road with gradual gradients making for easy going cycling, particularly suitable for families, although there are some short steeper sections giving more of a challenge.

Several partner organisations have been involved in taking the project forward including Aberdeenshire Council, Aberdeen City Council, Cairngorms National Park, Scottish Natural Heritage, Scottish Enterprise Grampian and Sustrans. Key to the success of the project has been the support of local landowners and communities along the way.

Note from the author:

This book shows the route as it runs from Aberdeen, heading out west to Ballater and beyond, but there is no right way to enjoy it as it is well signed from both directions. The local information, points of interest and recommendations are intended to be of use any way you choose to spend your time in the area, whether you explore it in sections, or in one trip.

There are additional walks in each of the four main sections of the route, as well as the section on Braemar. These are suggestions for detours off the route which can be accessed directly from the path. The walks take you to two National Trust for Scotland castles, down to the river Dee to see one of the old ferry crossings, around lochs formed from ice age glaciers, a Pictish Cross, and a geological wonder. Others take you along part of the route the railway was planned to take beyond Ballater, and also within view of the UK's highest golf course, in Braemar.

Written predominately with walking in mind, this book also caters for various users and modes of transport on the path, with references that are also helpful for cyclists and of course a range of outdoor friendly and dog friendly establishments are suggested. Additional

resources and links to enhance your visit are referred to on page 19.

The Deeside Way stretches for 41 miles, and I would encourage you to take your time and savour it. You could walk it in 3-4 days, but if you can, allow at least a week or ideally longer to experience the city of Aberdeen as well as the many villages and towns that the route flows through. Having a chance to do the additional routes also gives an even greater sense of what makes this part of the world so unique.

Distances of the sections have been included but time estimates have not, apart from a rough guide for the additional walks. I think it varies so much from person to person, depending on the mode of transport and whether you take a detour. It can take longer if you stop for a coffee or to take photos, which I think makes it all the more enjoyable.

How to use this book:

This simple key has been created as a quick glance guide to highlights along the route. These are positioned at the top of each section. Please note that the maps trace the route and river, a visual representation of the Deeside Way. You can find the route distances in the titles, and the points of interest are marked in accurate locations. It would be useful to use these alongside assigned OS maps - numbers 406, OL59 and OL58 complete the route.

It is recommended to visit the social media accounts and websites of the businesses and organisations for current opening times and further information. Please also continue to refer to the website linked at the front of the book for blog posts, route developments, and other relevant updates.

COMPANION GUIDE KEY:

 Architecture & heritage
Route includes points of interest with historical or architectural significance.

 Refuel on the route
Tried and tested coffee and/or food stops to be found on these routes.

 Shop local
Independent retail stores and businesses are a bonus part of these sections.

 Into the woods
Enjoy forested sections during these routes.

 Additional walk
Wander off the Deeside Way and discover new paths, offering stunning scenery and new adventures!

 People of the Deeside Way
Stories from people who have lived or live on, use or work on the Deeside Way.

Visiting responsibly

As well as spending longer in the region, other considerations to be aware of to enjoy your visit safely and respect the environment and communities are:

- **OTHER USERS** The path is a social place, busier in some parts more than others - a path people use daily in many ways. Generally, my experience is that people are friendly in passing, especially on the more rural sections. There are several signs along the route encouraging courtesy in considering all users.

- **ACCOMMODATION & CAMPING** There are campsites at Ballater at the end of the route and in Braemar, which is also featured. In Scotland you can wild camp responsibly, and there are various other accommodation options too. VisitAberdeenshire, mentioned on the next page is a good resource for accommodation listings.

- **TOILETS** There are a number of cafés included in this book as recommendations, which make good stops to use the facilities if you are a customer. There are also some public toilets in the more populated villages, and these are highlighted throughout.

- **BE PREPARED** Although the route is not remote or too demanding, the Sustrans website reminds that walking and cycling routes change over time, and that weather conditions may also affect path surfaces. It advises to please use your own judgement when using the route based upon the weather and the ability, experience and confidence levels of those in your group.[11]

Further resources on enjoying the outdoors responsibly:

- Scottish Outdoor Access Code
  https://www.outdooraccess-scotland.scot/

- Leave No Trace - the 7 principles, which you can read more about on the website - https://lnt.org/

Enhance your visit

There are a number of resources, organisations, events and information sources available to enhance your experience of visiting the area, or enjoying the Deeside Way as a local. Some suggestions to refer to include:

- **VisitAberdeenshire** The destination management and marketing organisation (DMO) for the region provides a wealth of information for those visiting the area, and the website is a great resource. **www.visitabdn.com**

- **The Deeside Way website** The route's official website illustrates the route in detail and lists the various partner organisations involved in developing, funding and managing the route. **www.deesideway.org** Sustrans Route 195

- **Farmers Markets** If you can time your exploration of the Deeside Way on a weekend when there is a farmers' market taking place, it is a great chance to try out local produce and support local businesses. There are markets in Banchory, Aboyne, Ballater, and Braemar - The Ghillie's Larder. Aberdeenshire Council's website provides updates - search for 'farmers' markets'. **www.aberdeenshire.gov.uk**

- **Public Transport** Stagecoach operates the bus that runs between Aberdeen's Union Square bus station and Braemar, which is usually the number 201. More regular buses run between Aberdeen and Banchory, and also to Ballater, so it is best to check the website before travelling – **www.stagecoachbus.com**. Firstbus operates the number 19 bus, covering the city section too **www.firstbus.co.uk**. You can also check bus information at **www.travelinescotland.com**

Getting to the start of the path from the train and bus station in Aberdeen is included on page 22.

- **Cairngorms National Park** A big draw of the area is that the walk route leads you into the Eastern Cairngorms. There is a marker on the road before you approach the village of Dinnet, denoting the transition into the park– further mentioned in that section of the book. The visitor website for the park is **www.visitcairngorms.com**

- **Cycle Hire** There are a number of businesses along the route that repair and hire bikes, as well as some which offer guiding. Some individual businesses have been featured in the book and more information can also be found at **www.visitabdn.com/what-to-do/adventure-activities/cycling**

- **Festivals and Events** As well as the regular farmers' markets mentioned above, depending on the time of year you are in Aberdeen and Deeside, some of the towns and villages host festivals, from walking and cycling, to art exhibitions, literary events and Highland Games. **www.visitabdn.com/whats-on**

GETTING TO THE START - 1 MILE / 1.6 KM

If you travel into Aberdeen by rail or bus, you will arrive from the stations into Union Square Shopping Centre. The start of the Deeside Way at Duthie Park is about a 20-minute walk as described here (or 5 to 10-minute cycle).

Head out of the station onto Guild Street and stay to the left-hand side, heading across the overbridge. This is an interesting riveted and latticed steel bridge which may date from 1909, which is the date of the former suburban railway beneath it, or 1913 when the rest of Aberdeen Station was built.[12]

The towering BT offices emerge to the left, and at the end of the bridge follow the road round to the left onto College Street. Carry on straight ahead until you come to the College Street car park and cross the road onto the right-hand side of the street at either set of lights, before or after the car park entrance. Stop at the next crossroads, where there is a sign across the road pointing right towards the A93 to Braemar.

Cross the road to this sign – you are now on Wellington Place. At the next crossroads, take a left down Crown Street. Crown Street is now the main thoroughfare through a Conservation Area with simple styled granite buildings. When you reach the foot of Crown Street, you will see a sign with a pointing hand to your right across the other side of the road, onto Ferryhill Road. Follow this sign as the road curves round to the left and rises in a steady incline.

Ferryhill is also a city Conservation Area with a mixture of architectural styles, and interestingly, it was considered rural until the mid-19th century when the city expanded. The granite villas and grand buildings in this area make it a popular residential area and it easy to see why, especially on a sunny day when the gardens are in bloom and the mica in the granite is glistening.

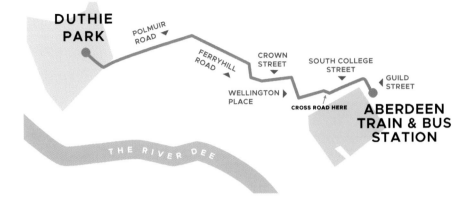

As you head further up the hill, you will see a terrace of quaint looking granite houses with a grassy area in front on your left. In the spring, this patch of grass is carpeted in crocuses. Heading up towards the church you will see a brown tourist sign pointing down to your left to the Duthie Park. This road is called Polmuir Road. Head down it as far as you can see, there are some more lovely granite buildings to look at.

Passing a bright red post box, the road heads to the left into Deemount Terrace, but you should stay on Polmuir Road. There is a nice pub and hotel on the Terrace called 'Inn at the Park' which is family and dog friendly. There are several guest houses and accommodation in this area as an option to stay nearby before starting the route.

Heading towards the park entrance, you will see the impressive gate posts and a gate house - and the Duthie Park car park. You can go into the park through the gates but to get to the start of the Deeside Way, take a right from the car park into a further parking area, past a grassy bank on your right - another patch which is blanketed with crocuses in the spring. You should find an interpretation board for the start of the Deeside Way. *Enjoy the journey.*

DUTHIE PARK

Situated on the north side of the river Dee and covering 44 acres, the Duthie Park was opened in 1883. It was presented to the city by Miss Elizabeth Crombie Duthie of Ruthrieston and laid out at a cost of £50,000.[13] Now called *The David Welch Winter Gardens*, which are well worth a visit, the original Palm House or Winter Gardens were built in 1899.

Image courtesy of Aberdeen City Libraries/The Silver City Vault

The indoor gardens were renamed in 2002 in memoriam of one of the most influential parks directors in Aberdeen. David Welch is credited with transforming the city's parks and gardens during the 22 years he held this position.[14]

There are various areas to see, including the Temperate House, Corridor of Perfumes, Fern House, Victorian Corridor, Japanese Garden, Tropical House, and Arid House, which has one of the largest collections of Cacti and Succulents in Britain and the world's only talking cactus! Many generations now have childhood memories of visiting Spike over the years and throwing coins at McPuddock - the mechanical frog.

the
deeside
way

Scoffy Car Par

Scoffy Hill Trail

195 Deeside Way

SECTION 1:

Aberdeen to Drumoak

DRUMOAK   WEST CULTS

ABERDEEN

Aberdeen to Drumoak

10.6 MILES / 17 KM - EASY

This section is very varied as greenery and granite merge, passing through the leafy west end of the city into the suburbs, and finally out of the city bounds into the even more expansive spaces and farmlands of Aberdeenshire.

Crossing over the Holburn Bridge and towards Cults, notable points include Boxcar Coffee & Yard, an optional detour to Nan Shepherd's house, Newton Dee Camphill Community at Bieldside and the Heritage Centre at Culter, before heading towards the village of Drumoak.

Duthie Park to West Cults

3.5 MILES / 5.6 KM - EASY

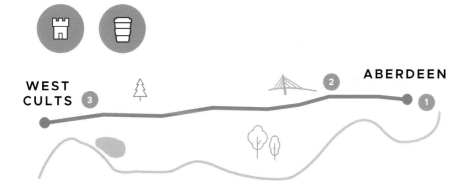

POINTS OF INTEREST:

1. Duthie Park (see page 24)
2. Holburn Bridge
3. Boxcar Coffee & Yard

1 **Duthie Park** The Deeside Way starts from the scenic surroundings of the Duthie Park, outside the park gates at Polmuir Road. Directions on how to get there from the train and bus stations in Aberdeen are on page 22, with some background information on the park and the famed Winter Gardens on page 24. There is an interpretation panel and mileage marker behind the winter gardens that signal the official start of the route.

The glasshouses of the winter gardens pass by on your left as you set off along the path. This section, which is lined with several benches, is popular and often busy with dog walkers, cyclists, and runners, being close to the centre of the city. It is alive with birdsong and backs onto the lively urban gardens heading west from the city centre.

Passing under a road bridge, continue along the path, and just under half a mile west of the park is the Allenvale Cemetery on your left, described as *'the final resting place of several of Aberdeen's most important and influential people'*.[15]

HOLBURN

2 **Holburn Bridge** Arriving at the site of the old Holburn Station, the platform remains are still very evident. There is another interpretation panel with some interesting snippets of information about how Holburn Street got its name and explaining that Holburn Station closed in April 1937 with the original bridge over the street being demolished in 1981. The new one opened in 2004, and the design concept was originated by students from the Scott Sutherland School of Architecture, Robert Gordon University (RGU)[16] - a short distance from this point.

There are a couple of access points on your right before the bridge, and a sign signalling it is six miles to Peterculter. Horse riders are asked to dismount crossing the bridge, as with several other bridges on the route.

Continuing for a straight section after the bridge, there is plenty to observe, from birches and blackbirds to benches and bird boxes.

RUTHRIESTON

Anderson Drive is a busy dual carriageway and walking under it has a contrasting mood with the urban atmosphere of its graffiti art as you go under the bridge. Several access paths on and off the route can be seen here. There is another stretch with a bench as you come into Ruthrieston, where you will see a green metal gatepost on your left.

Passing under the next pedestrian access bridge, if you glance up at it you will notice the sign of *James Abernethy & Co Engineers Aberdeen* who supplied the ironwork for a number of bridges in the area, as well as further afield in the UK, and a machine James Abernethy engineered even went as far as Australia – a large lathe made for turning granite columns.[17]

GARTHDEE

Following straight on, passing under Auchinyell Road bridge and then another pedestrian access bridge, the path leads you into the Garthdee area. There is a post which signs left to the RGU Garthdee campus, one and ¾ miles away, and again there are green metal gates like those at Ruthrieston.

Further along on this section, you will come to a minor crossroads, with the route continuing straight on. More benches line this stretch, and it starts to move away a little from the more built-up residential area, transitioning between Garthdee and Pitfodels. As you reach the end of a housing section, on your right there is a small access path through some staggered metal gates which leads up to the main A93 road, which has bus access.

PITFODELS

The more fertile and greener feel of this part is enhanced by the allotments to your left, with over 100 'plotters' working full, half or micro allotments on the site, managed by the Garthdee Field Allotments Association in partnership with Aberdeen City Council.[18]

Another waymarker post signs left towards Garthdee and RGU, then passing under a road bridge with access points, there is an interpretation board announcing you have arrived at Pitfodels Station.

There are some interesting fragments of information to read, from the possible Gaelic origins of the name 'Pitfodels', to the surrounding wildlife habitat.

'In the spring and summer many species of birds nest here, collecting greenfly and other 'bugs' from the nearby allotments and gardens. On warm summer evenings look out for pipistrelle bats out hunting for mosquitos and other insects to feed on.'[19]

The board also tells of Pitfodels Castle, a medieval motte and bailey castle made of wooden construction. Its site lies to the south of the station and all that exists now is the earth mound. Remnants of the old platform wall line the path at the station, and the building is now a private house.

Past Pitfodels, this stretch increasingly opens out, feeling calmer and quieter as fields emerge to your left and right. Birch line the path, which are even more striking on a day when the sun reflects off their bark. *It is hard to ignore the wealth of this area as striking new builds and more traditional statuesque granite homes sit side by side.*

CULTS

A little further along you will pass under another overbridge, with further access points on and off the path. This section is often busier as you are now approaching the former Cults Station. It was speculated in the local press in November of 2021 whether an elusive artist had possibly visited the area with the headline, '*Has Banksy come to visit?*'[20] following the discovery by two walkers of an artwork appearing on a building along the Deeside Way at this point. The graffiti painting is of a child holding up a sign with the caption, '*contribution to society stands on principal of love*'.

A welcome sight is when the board is out signalling that the takeaway café is open, which occupies part of the old station site.

③ **Boxcar Coffee & Yard** This is a takeaway café that was established in 2020, and is open seven days a week for cakes, scones, soup, toasties, bacon rolls, and of course, coffee. A dog friendly spot with water bowls and a warm welcome, the café has also recently installed tables and benches outside at this prime stop along the path.

{insta} @boxcarcoffeeandyard {fb} /boxcarcults

The city bounds have expanded much further out of town over the past century, with Cults having once been considered rural. The image below from the Silver City Archive is believed to be from around 1940 and was taken from the back of the station, showing the open fields that once surrounded it. The railway of course being one of the contributing factors in the growth of this suburb.

Another image from 1920 shows the station in operation and the sign which is still visible on the platform. Its distinct platform edges, and the rail themed café make the heritage connections at this station more prominent than some others.

Images courtesy of Aberdeen City Libraries/The Silver City Vault

PEOPLE OF THE DEESIDE WAY
Crawford Paris

Aberdeen resident and photographer Crawford Paris shares what the Deeside Way means to him...

"There is sanctuary in the Deeside Line, perhaps somewhat surprisingly at its very beginnings in Aberdeen. Here, the green strip transports you from the granite lined streets to a welcome leafy haven. It is a pleasant escape that, along with the River Dee, I find myself being drawn to more often than the city's golden shore.

From Aberdeen, the Deeside Line, accompanied by its meandering companion, provides the tantalising feeling of connection, not just to the towns and villages along it, but to the vast area surrounding the Cairngorms. When city life overwhelms, being on the Deeside Line and trundling west for just half an hour has the ability to make you feel crucially closer to the open wilderness it spans out to.

For me, the stretch embarking from Aberdeen is as much about a mental connection to these faraway places as a physical one, and it never ceases to provide."

{insta} @crawford.paris

The Cults Station interpretation board is worth a read, again providing some gems of information; about the area being prone to flooding, the growth of Cults due to the railway 'subbie' commuter service, the *'Shakkin Brigge'*, and a poem, written in Doric - an extract from *The Railway* by John Clark.[21]

A little way along from the station is a green sign pointing you to a winding pedestrian walk down to your left. There is a red dog waste bin, and opposite that on the right is an access point up to the road, passing a row of attractive granite houses. This is the access path you would take if you want to visit the range of shops and amenities at Cults, including the independent and dog friendly café called Blether. You take a right at the top of this path up Station Road to the A93.

On the Deeside Way, the next thing you will come up to is an underpass at the section where Station Road goes overhead. This is a leafy stretch, full of colourful rhododendron flowers in the spring.

WEST CULTS

You will come up to another minor crossroads with a sign down to the left for Allan Park, but the Deeside Way continues straight on. Benches on your left are a nice chance to pause with a lovely viewpoint overlooking the valley. Here you approach a green metal footbridge, which again offers charming views over to the left, and you are now at West Cults. Although not officially a station, West Cults was a 'halt' used by the 'subbies' – suburban commuter trains – for 43 years.[22]

Just past the bridge on the right is an optional extra route up to the home of Nan Shepherd, which is marked with a plaque. Continuing on the Deeside Way is on page 46.

Paying Homage to Nan Shepherd

This is a short detour off and back on the path at this spot, taking around 10-20 minutes in total (if walking) to visit the commemorative plaque marking the home of writer and poet, Nan Shepherd. Probably best known for her 'mountain memoir', *The Living Mountain*, and featuring on the Scottish £5 bank note since 2016.

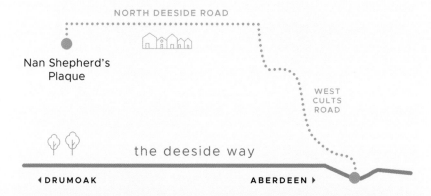

Leaving the Deeside Way at West Cults just after the green bridge, turn right at the green metal barrier and head through a small car park. As you come to a road turn left and follow that road up as it curves round to the left and then right. One of the last times I walked in this spot a red squirrel ran across the road in front of me.

This takes you up to the North Deeside Road (A93), which can be quite busy at times so take care along this section. Turn left at the main road and keep to the left as you walk along the pavement for approximately 150 metres, until you come to the plaque on the wall at number 503 North Deeside Road. Whilst you cannot see a lot from here, respecting the privacy of the current occupants, you can get a sense of where she lived, where she wrote, and her base to explore from.

Images courtesy of the Estate of Nan Shepherd.

The commemorative plaque is mounted at the entrance to 'Dunvegan'. It is a visible reminder of Nan's contribution to Scottish literature, her having been described as 'one of Scotland's finest novelists of the early twentieth century'. To find out more about Nan Shepherd's life, I would highly recommend reading *Into the Mountain: A life of Nan Shepherd*, a biography by Charlotte Peacock.

Kerri Andrews in her book *Wanderers - A History of Women Walking* beautifully describes the connection between Nan Shepherd and the river Dee...

"The waterways of the Cairngorms held a particular power for Shepherd, perhaps because they often emerged from the dark and secret places that she so enjoyed exploring, but perhaps also because she lived almost all her life alongside the Dee, the mightiest river to which the mountains give birth high on the plateau between Cairn Toul and Braeriach. The village of Cults on the eastern edge of Royal Deeside, just outside Aberdeen and the flat land of the river's estuary, is many miles from the windswept, rain-scoured mountainside 4,000 feet up from which the Dee first emerges, but for Shepherd, there was an integral affinity between the two, a recognisable and tangible kinship. With her home on the river, Shepherd had a visible link to the high places to which she loved to go – the waters that ran past her house had emerged, however many weeks or months or years earlier, from the falls or pools at the heart of the massif."[23]

Wanderers - A History of Women Walking by Kerri Andrews, Copyright © Kerri Andrews 2020. Reproduced with permission of the Licensor through PLSclear

As the plaque is on the A93 road, there is bus stop access here. To get back on the Deeside Way, retrace your steps, turning right onto West Cults Road and following it back round to the path, turning right at the minor substation back to the path.

West Cults to Drumoak

7.1 MILES / 11.4 KM - EASY

DRUMOAK

WEST CULTS

POINTS OF INTEREST:

4 Newton Dee Camphill Community

5 Aberdeen Western Peripheral Route (AWPR) Viewpoint

6 St. Peter's Heritage Centre (Culter)

7 View of Belskavie Tower

BIELDSIDE

Back on the Deeside Way, there are six miles to go at this point to Drumoak. Passing Deeside Golf Club on your left, which opened in 1903, there is another bench and a lovely viewpoint overlooking the course. As you near the old station at Bieldside, platform walls begin to emerge at the edge of the path, with another interpretation board telling of the members of the golf club being issued with special rate tickets for use on the railway when it was active, and before car ownership became more common.

It also tells of the wildlife habitats around this section, with bird and bat boxes in the trees, and brambles and nettles providing homes and food for butterflies, blackbirds, song thrushes and small mammals. Referring to the upcoming section where the railway went through a cutting, it suggests that in spring the ditches on either side of the track are alive with frogspawn and tadpoles.[24]

You will then come along to another green metal overbridge, where there are a set of steps just past the bridge on your right. These will take you up to Golf Road and up to the Bieldside shops on the A93. The overbridge is the road access to the golf club, so take care if you use the steps when you come out on this access road.

There are various amenities at Bieldside, the name coming from Gaelic, meaning 'the sheltered side'.[25] Two places to mention are a bike workshop and speciality coffee shop called Ground and the Bieldside Inn, a restaurant and bar which is also dog friendly. If you do head up at this point, you can retrace your steps back down Golf Road and back down the steps to the Deeside Way.

Back on the path, this is a very lush, green section in the summer with birch and ivy surrounding the path. It also seems to attract birds year-round and is full of life whatever season you experience it in. The next overbridge you come to is likely to have a sign about Newton Dee store, somewhere I would recommend visiting as it is a very special place with a peaceful atmosphere.

Just before the overbridge there is a red dog waste bin on your left at the entrance to a steeper trodden path up the bank up to your left. This will take you up to Newton Dee Community. Coming through a little wooden gate covered in ivy, this leads on to a minor access road. Turn left and then you will shortly see signs on the right for the Newton Dee Store and a map of the village.

④ Newton Dee Camphill Community Camphill is a charity that supports adults with learning difficulties and other special needs, to create meaningful work and community. There is an excellent health food store, gift shop and café, which are run as a social enterprise and generally open Tuesday - Saturday. It is suggested to check the website in advance to confirm current opening hours. **www.newtondee.co.uk**

Retrace your steps back through the wooden gate and down the bank onto the Deeside Way. There are another couple of overpasses to go under for minor road access above, as you continue on. There is so much birch here, especially on the left side of the track, as the path moves away from the more densely populated areas, feeling more open with fields on both sides and benches to rest and enjoy the peace along this stretch.

MURTLE AND MILLTIMBER

Passing over a footbridge at Camphill Community, you are now approaching Murtle Station. There is one of the official interpretation boards again, and evidence of the platform walls quite far along here. The former station is now a private residence. Murtle get its name from the Gaelic 'Mor-tulach' – the great knoll (a small hill or mound) and Murtle is mentioned as early as 1163 when the Barony of Murtle was granted by Malcolm IV to the Bishop of Aberdeen.[26]

A slightly surprising sight perhaps, but one that always makes me smile, are the alpacas you are likely to see on your left near the interpretation boards. These are part of the Camphill Community, which you can find out more about at **www.camphillscotland.org.uk**.

Further out of town at this point, it softens into the spaciousness of the surrounding fields, and the quietness. The birch is sparser here, allowing light to get through more easily, especially on a bright day. You will come along to an access path on your right with an option to take you up to the main road (A93). Continuing on the path, you will pass through an underpass and past a viewpoint bench. There is a T-bar sign signalling this point is five miles to Drumoak and five miles from the Duthie Park.

Old iron posts from the days of rail are noticeable here, with an opening and a visible path down to your left. Although not a specific walk, you can head down this way to get to the river Dee, which would take around 20 minutes there and back on foot. I would not recommend veering too far off route here, but I understand the pull of wanting to see the water. The walk back is on a bit of an incline, and you may see some Shetland ponies as you head back to the Deeside Way.

Coming along to the equestrian paddock, you will then go under an overpass which is the access road to the equestrian centre. This is a picturesque section, especially if you like horses, as there are vast

fields opening out on your left as the path approaches the bypass (AWPR), and there are benches to stop at along the way.

When I first walked the complete route, it was not long before the bypass opened. Walking over an empty dual carriageway felt like a scene from a film. Opening in February 2019, it is now a busy road which you are likely to hear in the distance before you reach it, but it is not imposing.

There are a couple of further viewpoint benches for alternative stopping options. Look out for a green metal barrier gate on your right with another Deeside Way interpretation board and a notice to head off the obvious path to remain on the Deeside Way route. It is easy to keep going straight on, which I have done more than once…

5 **AWPR** Take a left, along a road for a short distance, then you will see a small sign to go over the bridge of the bypass (Aberdeen Western Peripheral Route). For those without a head for heights, you will likely want to get across swiftly, although there are high barriers, but it is quite remarkable to see the busy road activity passing and think about what is below your feet. It makes for an interesting viewpoint.

At the end of the bridge, you will come out at another busy road, which does have a pavement. Keep on the left-hand side until you see a green metal gate and route signs on the opposite side of the road - cross over to continue the Deeside Way.

CULTER

This is another marked stretch with silver birch on the left, and more fields of horses as it approaches Peterculter - or Culter as it is known, and as the station was called. A calm and quiet section, often with several birds around, I have spotted a bird of prey in this area more than once but have not been able to get close enough to identify it.

At Pittengullies crossover, you go down and up crossing the road, and then continue straight on. This is well signed with route posts, indicating there are four miles to go until you reach Drumoak. A lovely viewpoint bench I would recommend stopping at, even briefly, looks out over the Dee and offers a welcoming message in Doric: It says, '*Come and rest for a wee whiley*' – how could you refuse…?

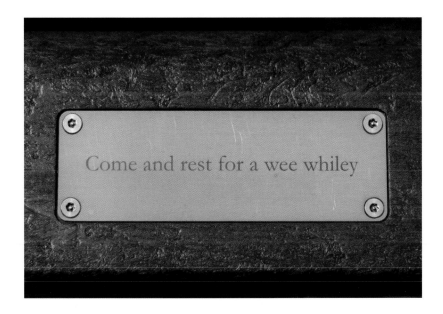

It is nice to walk with the river to your left and you see it meandering away from you as you get closer to the old Culter Station. The platform is visible on your right from quite a distance, it being the best-preserved station in the city, and the last one to close in December 1966. As you walk towards the station site, there are several benches overlooking the river and the Peterculter Churchyard, inviting you to take a moment and appreciate the surroundings.

At the far end of the platform the large Culter Station sign is noticeable on your right, with the interpretation board opposite, detailing more history on the background of the station and it being used as an important freight station serving the Culter paper mill, which closed in 1981.

It also describes the possible wildlife you could spot in this area, and mentions buzzards, which may have been what I previously spotted. It also suggests you may be able to see roe deer, foxes, a variety of butterfly species, and waxwing birds that visit from Scandinavia during the winter.[27] I would recommend stopping to read these station boards, with this being the last in the city boundaries. They do not continue in the same format as you head into Aberdeenshire.

6 **St. Peter's Heritage Centre** The St. Peter's Heritage Centre down on your left is a place to find out more about this area's history and heritage. The former church is now home to a series of exhibitions, featuring the Culter Paper Mill, farming in Aberdeenshire, Rob Roy, and a model and track of the Deeside Railway Line, as well as other local exhibits.

The Heritage Hall next door started off life as a chapel or 'Iron Kirkie' in Ballater, and was brought to Culter by rail in 1907. The hall is now used by local groups and is sometimes open for teas and coffees. **www.culterheritage.org**

It is a little less obvious where the Deeside Way continues at this point, but there are some small signs to look out for. There is also the option to head up to the main A93 road via Station Road, which is behind the Culter Station sign and past the red coloured house, then turn left on the main road if you want to visit any of the shops at Culter. There is a dog friendly coffee shop called Neil Selbie & Co., and an ice cream shop called 'Fit's the Scoop', a library, and other conveniences. Retrace your steps if you take this detour back to the Culter Station sign.

To continue on the Deeside Way, look out for a white wall on the corner of Howie Lane and Station Road East, the gable end of a building with a hydrant marker on it, and a small Deeside Way marker above that directing you left (as you are facing it). Follow this road round, keeping to the left for a short distance, before you see a route waymarker post on the right where a track veers uphill to the right. It indicates that it is three miles to go at this point to Drumoak.

TO DEESIDE WAY

EVERY TIME YOU HAVE THE COURAGE
TO SPEAK OUT AGAINST TYRANNY
YOU GIVE ANOTHER PERSON
THE COURAGE TO DO THE SAME

This section continues on the original railway track, and is again lined with silver birch. There are a few houses to pass, and this section gets more open again, with a bench first on the left, and then on the right. This bit of path is narrower and more winding – prone to being muddy if there has been wet weather. A marker will veer you slightly to the right and railway sleepers edge the track on the left, with another sign signalling to go straight on. The remains of the fencing made from sleepers goes on for a long distance here, and there is something quite artistic about the broken remnants, especially if you time it to see the sun shining through the gaps.

Coming up to a minor four-way crossroads, there is a sign on the left side fence posts saying 'footpath' – here you continue straight on. The fields make this farming area feel vast and it is a section you will feel a little more 'away from it all' than others as it transitions from town to country - from Aberdeen city into Aberdeenshire.

Coming to a barrier with clear signs to head round to the right, with more Deeside Way markers, a tower will come into view in the distance over on the right.

7 **View of Belskavie Tower** 'Mysterious Belskavie Tower', as it is referred to, is reputed to have been a watch-tower for Drum Castle and possibly the site of a signal station for the Romans at the nearby Normandykes Roman camp.[28] The tower *(pictured below)* is situated in Newmill Woods, managed by Forestry and Land Scotland.

Come up the track here approaching a road, and there is another Deeside Way post indicating to turn left. Although a minor road, be careful of traffic as the road here is very narrow and visibility can be poor on some of the corners.

This is the main section of the Deeside Way which is on a road - walking this section takes around 10 minutes. You will come to a marker post instructing you to turn into the road to your left, where the Coalford Canine Retreat is on your left. Follow the road round, which is still a minor road, but it should be even quieter. Continue straight on.

Heading towards Drumoak

This bit has an interesting feel in that is seems remote, but you actually carry on this quiet, minor road for quite a distance. Along this stretch you will catch your first glimpse of Clachnaben in the distance. Clachnaben is a 589-metre hill, with a distinctively shaped large granite tor at its peak.

Passing a few tracks on your left, after a stretch you will see a Deeside Way triangular sign which appears before coming to a few houses on your right. You will soon approach a crossroads at Dalmaik. The Deeside Way continues by going straight ahead, described from paragraph two on page 64, but there is an additional optional walk here to Drum Castle, which is to your right at this point.

Drum Castle

3.2 MILES / 5.2 KM - EASY

Allow an hour for walking there and back, plus allow extra time to explore the estate, café, castle and gardens.

Drum is an impressive castle of several eras, composed of a medieval tower, a Jacobean mansion, and a Victorian extension - making it a very intriguing place to explore over 700 years of history.

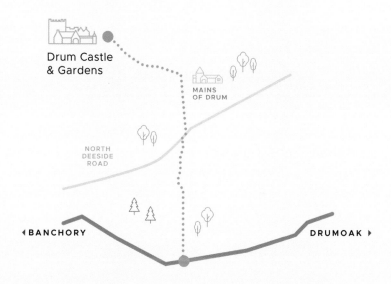

Taking a right at the Dalmaik crossroads, this is a long stretch of minor road, with woodland on either side. As you reach the end of the wooded section, you will pass a few houses on the right and fields which often have horses.

Heading up and over a road bridge, there are more houses on the right and a sign to Drumoak Kitchens, but continue straight ahead, being mindful of cars, tractors and other farm traffic, as again, some of the corners can make visibility a little more challenging. There is a Scottish Society for the Prevention of Cruelty to Animals (SSPCA) centre further up this road on your right. When you can see the centre, head onto a narrow path which leads up to a bus stop. You are going to cross the main road here so take care as cars can be going fast and again, visibility is not ideal.

Once you have crossed the A93, you will see a sign straight ahead of you pointing up the road ahead to Drum Castle, marked as a single-track road with passing places by a blue sign. If walking, at this point turn right towards the bus stop, a short distance along and you will see a track up to your left, going in the same direction as the road. Turn to go up there to save you walking on the road. You can also get a bus here to head back into Aberdeen.

The walking track runs through the grounds of the Mains of Drum Garden Centre, to your right. The garden centre also has an area for locking up bikes outside, and picnic benches. With its impressive turret and 5-star visitor attraction accreditation from VisitScotland, Mains of Drum is a high quality, independent garden centre. I would recommend it for a browse at the lovely gifts, homewares, and plants. It also has a restaurant which you can pop into for a relaxed coffee and a cake, or something more substantial.

Continuing on the walking track as it veers closer to the road, past a dog waste bin, follow this path until you come up to a gate. Be careful coming out of the gate as you are suddenly on the road again, and at a blind corner. Cross over to the signs for Drum Castle and Estate, on to the driveway. This is edged with beautiful snowdrops around March time, and the estate always has something to offer in each season. The driveway is also lined with pictures of wildlife on the estate, speed limits, and snippets of the historical themes in the castle.

Continue walking along the driveway for a good distance until the castle emerges on the left.

Its striking 'Old Tower' is the first façade of the building you see, before you reach the entrance to the later Courtyard addition. The tower was given to the Irvine family along with the Royal Forest by Robert the Bruce in 1323.[29] The castle has undergone several transformations in its long history and twenty-four generations of the Irvine family lived here. It is now cared for by the National Trust for Scotland (NTS).

This is a multi-faceted, beautiful place, with walled gardens, walking routes, a café and also changing exhibitions within the castle itself. The library is particularly striking, which sits behind the arched window you can see in the old tower - home to approximately 4,000 books.

The word Drum comes from the Gaelic word *druim*, meaning ridge – with the estate being positioned on a ridge. You can find out more about the castle, estate and its varying opening times throughout the year at **www.nts.org.uk/visit/places/drum-castle**. It also has close links with Crathes Castle, another NTS castle, which is featured in an additional walk on page 76.

63

Once you are ready to head back to the Deeside Way, make your way back down the driveway, reading the signs on the reverse, and seeing the scenery from a different view. Take care crossing back over to the gate into the Mains of Drum Garden Centre grounds, and follow the path back down to the A93 main road. Crossing that, you will head back the way you came, past the SSPCA centre on your left this time, and back along the road to the Dalmaik crossroads on the Deeside Way, where you will turn right to continue on the route.

Carry on along this minor road, staying to your right when you come to a marked private farm entrance - there is a post here at the corner to direct you. You are on this road for a short while, passing a house on your right, and then straight ahead you will see it turn into a smaller track again, at the point where the road veers sharply round to the right. This track will take you onto the off-road Deeside Way path, signalled by another post.

This section was re-surfaced in 2021, and is renowned for the large number of rabbits in this area. There is also a high chance of spotting a red kite in this vicinity too, and the distinctive shape of the hill Clachnaben also becomes clearer on this section.

The obvious path ambles round fields either side, following along until you approach a small number of houses. There is another Deeside Way marker and small wooden post, marking the end of this re-surfaced section and veering round to your left along a driveway track where you come up to a crossroads. Head straight on and you will spot another Deeside Way post.

This post is followed by another a little further along the path, which directs you round to the left, and as you head down this section, you will spot a bench on your right and then a there is a bit of a surprise carved in wood…

Curving to the right, you will head straight on for a stretch here, often lined with ferns, and not too far from the river again to your left.

There is a large grassy area here on the left known as 'the glebe' which would be a nice place to have a break and make use of the picnic benches.

In the corner of the glebe, which meets up with the path, you will see a gate, beyond which continues the Deeside Way. This is a more shaded spot, with dense forest to your left, as you head along and meet up with a minor road. As you reach the road, and look down to your left, you may get a glimpse of the Park bridge. This was built by Great North of Scotland Railway (GNSR) to facilitate access to Park Station for those living on the south side of the river.[30] It is currently not open for vehicle access.

The Deeside Way continues up to the right on the narrow path which runs parallel to the road, as indicated by more Deeside Way posts. This meanders back up towards the A93, passing by a lovely birch wood on your right, then up past Dee Valley Caravans. If you glimpse over to the office, part of this building had originally been Park Station, and you can still see the original chimney breasts.

As you come to the main road, you will see another post, and you take a left here. There is a bus stop across the road for access back into Aberdeen, or along on the left side of the road to go further out west into Deeside.

Drumoak to Banchory

DRUMOAK

MILTON OF CRATHES

BANCHORY

Drumoak to Banchory

7.3 MILES / 11.8 KM - EASY

This is a varied section which moves further into rural Deeside, offering particular points of interest at Park and Milton of Crathes, home to a variety of interesting local shops and the Royal Deeside Railway. There is also another beautiful tower house and estate to visit at Crathes Castle on an additional walk, as well as a scenic approach to all the amenities in the larger town of Banchory.

Drumoak to Milton of Crathes

4.2 MILES / 6.8 KM - EASY

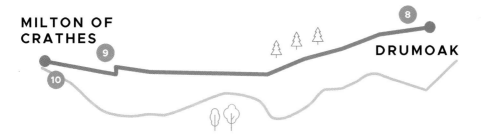

POINTS OF INTEREST:

8 Park Shop

9 Crathes Signal Box

10 Milton of Crathes & Hidden Scotland Shop

DRUMOAK AND PARK

Continue walking along the A93 through the village of Drumoak, past the east entrance to Park estate on your left, and you will notice a change to 40 miles-an-hour road signs as you enter Park.

Not far beyond that is another Deeside Way post directing onto the smaller path down to the left, which veers away from the road a little, along fields on your left, and past a small number of allotments and buildings on your right.

8 **Park Shop** As you come to another post, you will see Park Shop to your right through an opening in the trees. For lovers of great coffee, artisan local produce, delicious pastries and hot pies in stylish surroundings, Park shop is a must visit. If you do head over to visit the shop, take care crossing the road as cars can be going quite fast at this point.

This is not your average corner shop. Having opened in 2018, it has become a favourite of cyclists, walkers, locals and day trippers. Outside there is seating and tables round the back, as well an adorable little Park Shop Library, which quotes, *"reading one book is like eating one potato chip"* (which you can also buy inside). A nice addition to borrow or donate some reading material, adding even more charm to this quaint village store.

{insta} @park.shop.park   {fb} @parkshopdrum

PARK SHOP

Free Library

"Reading one book is like eating one potato chip"

Please help yourself to a book and return after you are done.

Back on the Deeside Way, this is a nice stretch to take in the surroundings and changing seasons. The path is quite near to the main road for this section, but there are plenty of scenic distractions to draw your attention away from it. The fields to the left often have livestock and it looks especially lovely here when there is sunlight dappled through the trees. This is often a quieter section of the route too, between Drumoak and Crathes.

Coming up to a bridge on the route of the old railway line, there is a notice asking for cyclists and horse riders to dismount. A number of houses painted in 'estate green' which are part of the Park Estate with the lands to the left of this section. Park Estate is now private, having been sold from the Irvines of Drum in 1737, the family previously mentioned on page 61 in relation to Drum Castle, and has frequently changed owners since.[31]

You will cross a number of access tracks into the Park Estate as you continue on this section, which is an obvious path with varying wooden posts, blue signs on fences and gates, and round symbols on other posts or markers. Passing Park Smiddy on your right, you then enter a darker and more densely covered bit of path with remnants of gates from the railway, and another crossing into the Park Estate.

A good bit further along there is a second bridge asking for cyclists and horse riders to dismount once again as you come into the Netherpark Quarry entrance. Take care crossing, and continue straight ahead. There is a change in feel of the path here as it gets a little narrower and wilder, but is still close to the road. The landscape then opens up with more expansive views and scenery to the left, seeing over to the South Deeside Road in the distance.

Crossing another access track to a small number of houses, you will pass a couple of seats and then a bench. Everything feels quite lush in late summer here, with the bracken in full bloom and the rosebay willowherb adding a pink tone along the verges. The varying views and visibilities changes with the weather, seasons and time of year, which I think makes it even more interesting.

"The birch, for instance – from its February purple to its golden fall, bark, twig, sprinkled buds, catkins, early and late leaf – the birch by itself is a study in colour that provides endless delight."[32]

Nan Shepherd, on 'The Colours of Deeside'

As you head towards the Crathes junction, you will pass through many avenues of silver birch. Keep following the path as it curves around the side of a fence and then takes a fairly sharp right as you once again come up to towards the A93.

Follow a short distance along the main road, passing a number of striking houses, and depending on the time of year there are often wildflowers along the pavement here too. Take the next left turnoff along the road signed for 'Stonehaven' and there is a Deeside Way post. Walk down the 'slug road' as it is known, staying on the left side, and cross at the second island, signalled by another Deeside Way post.

Once you cross the road, follow the marker to re-join the Deeside Way path - up the side of a small access road on your right and a playpark and new housing development on your left. There are a few houses in this section as you turn round to the left following the main path, spotting another post here straight ahead. This section of the path opens up even more but also feels quite wild and intriguing.

CRATHES

⑨ **Crathes Signal Box** The Crathes Station signal box remains to the right, which closed in 1954 and the wooden top half was removed. Following the closure of the line, the station was owned for some years by the internationally acclaimed silversmith and engraver Malcolm Appleby. He rebuilt the upper section of the signal box to the original plans and there it sits today.[33]

The passenger platforms are just visible here, sitting alongside nature that has reclaimed this area. Interestingly, Crathes Station was originally a private halt for the Laird of Crathes (a castle which features as an additional walk on page 76) but became a public station in 1863 when the nearby Mills of Drum Station was closed.[34]

Continue on the path here, to the left past a memorial bench - you will soon see the St. Ternan's football fields emerge over to your left. Beyond them, you will head around an old stone cobbled bridge, and there is an option to do an additional walk up to Crathes Castle. If you are doing this walk, as described on the next page continue on under the underpass. For the Deeside Way, continued on page 82, take a left as signed by a marker post, then a right along towards Milton of Crathes.

Crathes Castle, Garden & Estate

2.4 MILES / 3.8 KM - EASY

Allow approximately an hour for walking up to the castle and back at a fairly leisurely pace, plus any extra time you want there to explore.

Slightly off the route, but easily accessible from the path is Crathes Castle. A 16th Century castle and visitor attraction, now cared for by the National Trust for Scotland (NTS), that I was lucky enough to volunteer and then work at several years ago.

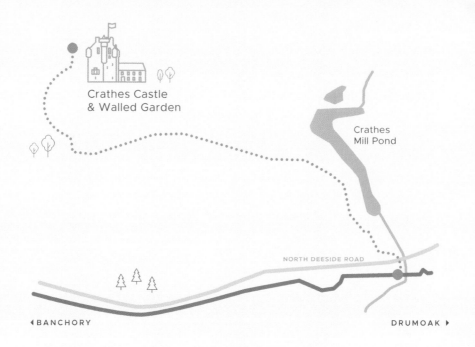

Crathes Castle
& Walled Garden

Crathes
Mill Pond

NORTH DEESIDE ROAD

◀ BANCHORY

DRUMOAK ▶

Once you are around the cobbled bridge you will see another Deeside Way post, and head right under the road underpass of the A93, coming up to meet the Crathes Castle Garden and Estate driveway. You will see the main entrance to your left for traffic, but take a right up towards the castle. Pass the gatehouse on your left, which is self-catering holiday accommodation, and just off the driveway to the left there is a track initially running alongside the road, with a white arrow and a sign marked 'main footpath to castle'. Take this path. You will pass a wooden carving of a heron, with the mill pond over to your right, which is beautiful and has several benches alongside it.

Follow the white marked trail, and over to your right you will see an historic driveway underpass, edged with iron railings. Further up the path, you will see more clearly over to the field on your right – called the Warren Field. This field is often home to Highland cattle (or coos) and in 2013, after an archaeological investigation, it was found to have evidence of the world's oldest lunar 'calendar', with remains even older than originally thought as the calendar was possibly created by hunter-gatherers about 10,000 years ago.[35]

Continue on the path until you come to a marker pointing you up to the right for the white trail. This is a slightly windier path with recent tree planting evident. You will see a small number of steps to go up (on the right at the top of the steps it signs you back the other way for the main gate footpath and East Trail) but go left and join another driveway, following this round where you will see another wooden carving - this time of a squirrel.

Heading along the driveway here, this is another charming castle approach, seeing it appear from between the trees, with the gardens and yew hedges visible on your right beyond the lawn. Crathes Castle is a classic Scottish tower house, with fairytale turrets and its own ghost story. The Burnett family, who lived in the castle for over 350 years, have roots in the area dating back to 1323 when Robert the Bruce granted them nearby land. Alexander Burnett built the castle in the 16th Century, an intricate maze of turrets, towers, oak panels and painted ceilings, many of which survive beautifully to this day.[36]

If you visit in October, you may be lucky enough to see the ivy which covers the castle entrance turning a rich deep red, which is one of my favourite times to be there.

There is a lot to see, including the walled gardens, or up the hill to the café, ticket office and shop. A number of other waymarked trails also line the estate, and you can see various notable trees which have their own interpretation markers, including the giant sequoia and the handkerchief tree.

The NTS is a conservation charity and cares for Crathes Castle, Garden and Estate. More information can be found at **www.nts.org.uk/visit/places/crathes-castle**

Once you are finished exploring, head back the way you came, down past the castle, signed for East Trail, back past the squirrel carving, and following the arrows for the white trail down parallel with the driveway until the gatehouse is visible again. Turn left beyond the gatehouse and before the main road, and back under the underpass of the A93. You'll see the Deeside Way marker again and walk back through the walls of what would have been a rail bridge, seeing the Deeside Way post again back where you started the additional walk near the cobbled bridge. Turn right here to reach the Milton of Crathes.

MILTON OF CRATHES

A point of interest on this part of the route where you may want to spend some time is Milton of Crathes.

10 **Milton of Crathes & Hidden Scotland Shop** Formed from a mill and steading blocks, and restored by the Leys Estate, this complex consists of varying independent businesses, several have changed in recent years but the art gallery has remained a constant, and there are new shops to discover, as well as an established brasserie, where you can also get takeaway coffees. This is an idyllic spot to be near the river, as well as to do some shopping.

MESOLITHIC DEESIDE

More evidence of the prehistoric past in this area was uncovered in 2021 when more than 1,200 Mesolithic tools were unearthed along the river here at Crathes.[37] More information on this continued research can be found at **www.mesolithicdeeside.org**.

The Hidden Scotland shop and planning station opened at Milton of Crathes in the summer of 2021. The Hidden Scotland brand is well known for its beautiful biannual magazine, weekly digital journal, strong social media presence, and web resources to showcase and inspire conscious travel to and within Scotland.

The shop reflects this quality brand and aesthetic and the planning station helps and inspires ongoing or future travels. Hand-selected products all created by Scottish makers feature within the shop.

{insta} @hiddenscotland + @hiddenscotlandshop

PEOPLE OF THE DEESIDE WAY
Karla Hall

Owner/Designer of Hidden Scotland Magazine and Shop, Karla Hall explains why Deeside was the perfect place to open a shop showcasing the variety & uniqueness of Scotland.

"The Milton of Crathes (located across the road from Crathes Castle), is an idyllic spot for Hidden Scotland to call its first home. This enchanting corner along the Deeside Way holds a lot of history dating back to the 17th Century, and today, we occupy the former Sawmill and Sawmill Cottage, where many of the original features remain, including the waterwheel.

The Sawmill and Cottage - now our studio space, gift shop, and planning corner- are cocooned in amongst the trees where we are treated to the sounds of the river flowing just outside our front door, which is accompanied by the chirps and whistles of the birds. Bliss!

Collectively this forges the ideal setting for us to house a curated selection of gifts made by designers and makers across Scotland and to share our planning station with visitors in order to showcase what there is to see & do in the local area and beyond.

Our small community within this hidden corner of Royal Deeside includes an art gallery, play park, brasserie, fly fishing school, independent shops, as well as the Deeside Railway station."

Visit Hidden Scotland Shop's social media and website for information on opening times and workshops hosted in their studio space.
www.hiddenscotland.co

Milton of Crathes to Banchory

3.1 MILES / 5 KM - EASY

BANCHORY

MILTON OF CRATHES

POINTS OF INTEREST:

11 Royal Deeside Railway Visitor Centre

12 Ride Coffee House

13 King George V Park

14 Banchory High Street

11 **Royal Deeside Railway Visitor Centre** Across the car park from the shops at the Milton of Crathes, you will see an old Victorian station, which is the visitor centre for the Royal Deeside Railway Preservation Society. This was not the location of a station originally, and the building was from Oldmeldrum, but the preservation and restoration of a section of rail track gives a great insight into what the line was like in the 'golden age of steam'. The society, which is a charity and run by volunteers, has restored around one mile of track, which visitors can experience throughout the year on certain dates. The station is also a visitor centre with railway memorabilia and a shop.

MILTON OF CRATHES

BRITISH RAILWAYS

D2094

PEOPLE OF THE DEESIDE WAY
Shayne MacFaull

Volunteer at the Royal Deeside Railway, Shayne MacFaull gives an insight into these special locomotives and how the railways' revival keeps the area's history alive.

"Volunteering at the Deeside Railway appealed to me because I felt I could help towards keeping the history behind the line alive. I enjoyed reviving old rolling stock and helping overhaul the locomotives as required.

It was great learning from the older generation and seeing what knowledge and youthful determination combined could achieve.

Beautiful scenery and steam trains combined with enthusiastic and friendly volunteers makes for a great day out."

Find out more at **www.deeside-railway.co.uk**

To resume the Deeside Way route, head for the path to the left of the station, and to the right of a field entrance. This can be a more popular section of the route with a variety of users as it follows near to the main road of the A93 again on the approach to the town of Banchory.

Although I do enjoy cycling this section, my preferred way to really take in the surroundings mindfully and notice the detail along the way is by walking. As Erling Kagge says in his book *Walking*,

"This is the secret held by all those who go by foot: life is prolonged when you walk. Walking expands time rather than collapses it."[38]

This section can narrow a little when the ferns are in full bloom. It follows closely beside the railway track that the volunteers have restored, and with a view of the river down to the left, as well as a number of fishing huts and the Milton of Crathes event field, which hosts a variety of events and gatherings.

Much further along, cross an access track with white wooden gates which signal the end of this part of the rail track. Continue straight on as you enter into a more expansive and open section again, glimpsing the first views of Scolty hill and the tower landmark, built in honour of General William Burnett, at its top. You will notice a shortcut which has been trodden through with a nice bench viewpoint. At this spot you will also see further evidence of the work of the preservation society.

Arriving at a section with a small blue sign directing you to veer to the right to stay on the Deeside Way path, there is a chance to pop down to your left to get a nice view at an open section of the river. You may also spot some people fishing here too depending on when you are there. Head back to the main path to continue the Deeside Way.

Heading towards Banchory

Coming along to an access path on the right, maintained by Banchory Paths Association, this would take you out at the West Lodge access of Crathes Castle, with opportunities for bus stops on either side of the A93. This point also gives access to The Barn, a multi-arts venue with Buchanan's Bistro café just next door, and a store now selling items by local artists and makers, called Fold. This can be accessed by heading right up the Hill of Banchory East Road, then taking the first right, then right again and following the road round to The Barn. **www.thebarnarts.co.uk**

Continuing on the Deeside Way, this stretch gives an elevated view over the river with a few opportunities and paths to get down to the river itself. There is view a of Clachnaben's distinctive shape, passing the sawmill to your right with the noticeable scent of the timber.

A good bit further along past an access path signed to a Morrison's supermarket, you will see a fishing hut on the left with a red roof and waney edged cladding. This is at a bit of a crossroads which veers round to the right, and you will see a waymarker with various options. There is a Deeside Way post directing you round to the left, coming to a nice open grassy area with several benches and a viewpoint over the river and up towards Scolty hill.

St. Ternan's Kirkyard is over to the right (St. Ternan is the patron saint of Banchory). Beyond the kirkyard on the right is the granite ruin of a water tower used by the original rail station, and slightly further along the path, there is a wall to your left which is where the retaining wall was built for the station platform. There is a path below it called the 'Platties' which is signed further along on the left down some steps.

Follow the main path which eventually winds round to the right, with more posts to keep you on track. You will come to a post which directs to the left to continue on the Deeside Way under a walkway bridge. Straight ahead is a set of steps. For a slight detour and a coffee stop, I would recommend heading up these steps and turning right at the top. This is a minor access road, and you will see Ride Coffee House about 175 metres up ahead.

(12) Ride Coffee House Ride Coffee House features in the *Scottish Independent Coffee Guide* (5th edition), and rightly so. Established in 2018, as the name would suggest, it attracts a lot of cyclists as well as walkers, locals and four legged friends due to it being very dog friendly. A bright indoor space with the wood burner making it especially cosy in the winter, it also boasts a generous outdoor seating area. The menu changes regularly and there is always a wide selection of cakes, bakes, wraps and hot rolls here, making it an excellent stop to refuel just off the route.

{insta} @ridecoffeehouse {fb} /ridecoffeehouse

BANCHORY

The Deeside Way heads further towards the centre of the town, which opens out more onto some larger grassy areas. Coming along to another post, cross over a minor access road, and carry on across (slightly to your left) and head along that path as it curves round to the left. This path now joins up with the minor access road as it leads to a car park area with picnic benches, following the route of the railway.

13 **King George V Park** King George V Park was donated to the people of Banchory in the 1930s and is a nice place to take a break. It can be very busy at the weekend, especially on a warm day in summer. You will pass a Girl Guide hut on your right as you head towards a busier road (Dee Street).

There is post on your left-hand side at the corner but it is a little hidden as it is next to a larger council sign for the King George V Park and Pavilion, and the street sign across the road does not mention the Deeside Way, although it indicates that down to your left is the river Dee. If not visiting Banchory high street, continue the route, found on page 96.

14 **Banchory High Street** Access to Banchory shops and high street. Here is where you can turn right and head up to the high street in Banchory, or turn left to continue on the route.

Banchory is the largest town on the Deeside Way and has a lot to offer in terms of cafés, shops, and amenities. If you are in or around Banchory on the third Saturday of the month, the Banchory Farmers Market is on from 9am - 1pm in the Bellfield car park, which you pass very close by to on the route, and features a wide range of local food and drink. There are also public toilets in the Bellfield car park, just over to the right of the Deeside Way at the end of King George V Park.

Yeadon's bookshop is an independent bookshop which has been in Banchory since 2007 and is worth a visit. The bookshop is opposite the entrance to the Bellfield car park on Dee Street. I would also recommend visiting Scott Skinner Square off the high street, which has a shop called Studio 1, a social enterprise stocking works from local artists and makers. The square also boasts a library and information centre and several other independent shops.

Rail came to Banchory in 1853 when the town grew rapidly, and the line shut in 1966, with the station demolished in the 1980s. Two *Banchory Heritage Walks* books have been produced by Banchory & District Initiative, visit **www.visitbanchory.com** for further information. The second book is particularly lovely in that one of the routes encourages you to look up at the bells and finials of some of the notable buildings of the town (and suggests taking binoculars!). There is also a walk called *'Remembering the Railway'* which has a wealth of interesting history of the rail and rail buildings, and wonderful photos. The booklets can be purchased from Studio 1 in Scott Skinner Square and from Yeadon's of Banchory.

Falls of Feugh ¾ m
Scolty Hill 2¼ m

Public Toilets, Parks
Deeside Way, River Dee

Library, Museum
Tourist Information
Town Hall

SECTION 3:

Banchory to Aboyne

KINCARDINE O'NEIL

ABOYNE

BANCHORY

Banchory to Aboyne

15.8 MILES / 24.4 KM - MODERATE

This is a varied section that goes mostly 'off' the original railway line route, as you cross the river Dee to divert into the Scolty woods and forest trails, before coming round to Ballogie Estate and crossing back over the Dee again at Potarch Bridge. The next place you come to is Kincardine O'Neil, the oldest village on Deeside, with an additional walk down to the river Dee. Heading into the woods again at Dess, this track winds back down to the old rail track on the approach to Aboyne. There is a small section before Aboyne which is not officially on the route, which is explained further in that section.

Banchory to Kincardine O'Neil

9.7 MILES / 15.6 KM - MODERATE

POINTS OF INTEREST:

15 Crossing the Dee

16 Scolty Woodlands Viewpoint

17 The 'Shooting Greens'

18 Potarch & The Dinnie Stones

19 Kincardine O'Neil Village

Once you head towards the river Dee (left if you came out of the park area) cross the road and continue left passing a bowling green, putting green and tennis courts. You will see a Scout hut and totem pole – which has a sign explaining more about it.

Across the road you will see a sign for Banchory Lodge, an attractive riverside hotel beautifully situated by the Dee which offers a number of indoor and outdoor dining options.

To your right you will see an area with three interpretation boards and a bench which overlooks the river - *Discover Banchory on Foot*, *Pearls in Peril*, and *Life on the River Dee*. These share a range of information on walking and cycling routes around Banchory, work to secure the future of the freshwater pearl mussel in the river Dee, and more about the habitat, wildlife and commerce of the river – also signposting to further resources.

PEOPLE OF THE DEESIDE WAY
Cheryl & Rosie

Cheryl Roberts and her loyal pup Rosie are local to the Deeside Way and enjoy it in all its seasons. Cheryl also has a vocational connection to the Deeside Way; the restoration of the Tullich Kirkyard - a later point of interest on the route.

"I suppose you sometimes take it for granted but it is a path that winds right up the area that I call home and we jump on it here and there depending on where we are and how many sets of legs and paws we have with us.

Our section (Me and Rosie) stretches from Banchory to Crathes via the Burn of Bennie, a combination of main path, and informal tracks that branch off and re-join so we can always vary our meander, and the embankment dips down from time to time so Rosie can have a wee paddle in the river. I love that the riverbank varies over the seasons, the bluebells behind the timber yard are always a welcome sight in the spring.

I guess the paths and the river are like an ever-changing constant in our lives that we follow through the seasons. That is probably the thing I love the most, always something new but then reassuringly the same."

More about the Tullich Kirkyard can be found on page 153.

99

(15) Crossing the Dee Crossing the bridge over the well signposted 'River Dee' - your first crossing to the south side of the river. The bridge offers a sweeping view up and down the river and as you cross the bridge, I would suggest staying on the right-hand side. You will see gates and a gatehouse on your right to the Blackhall Estate, and past the gatehouse is where the steps continue the Deeside Way ahead of you, indicated by a post. Trying to cross the road on the opposite corner can be a little dangerous due to limited visibility.

Head up the steps and turn right where there is another post clarifying the direction. Be aware that you are walking along quite a narrow minor road for a fairly short section. This can be busy as it is the access road up to the popular Scolty hill and woodland trails, where the path also heads towards. In late winter into early spring, this section is likely to be scattered with snowdrops.

There is a section of pavement on your right for a short while, and then you veer round to the left and follow the road round - as indicated with another Deeside Way post - and signed for 'Auchattie', until you see a sign to the right for Scolty Trails and continue up the road to the car park. You will shortly see a green Forestry and Land Scotland sign **www.forestryandland.gov.scot** and there is another Deeside Way post on your left-hand side directing you straight on.

Arriving into the car park area, keep heading straight up to the start of the trails. There are interpretation boards with maps to your left, and the path continues straight aheads.

SCOLTY, BLACKHALL AND SLEWDRUM FORESTS

As you head up the main track, you will come to a sign for the Deeside Way, signalling to take a right. This section leads you through woodland on a wide forestry track, and a series of T shaped waymarkers guide you on where there is any ambiguity of which path to take. You are following the main forestry track, and this bit feels quite different being far away from the original railway route. It is slightly more challenging due to the long slow incline, but it rewards with charming woodland surroundings. Look out to your right for the views offered by gaps through the trees.

16 Scolty Woodlands Viewpoint You will come to a viewpoint bench tucked over to your right, which is a nice spot to take a breather.

Heading up another inclined stretch there is then a well signed fork to the left, with signs indicating you are now in Slewdrum Wood. This area is rich with lichen which apparently indicates good air quality.

17 The 'Shooting Greens' The route merges into a small car parking area - this is the remains of old township along the Military Road, reputedly where soldiers camped and practiced rifle shooting.[39]

Heading towards Potarch

A Deeside Way post indicates where to continue the path, to the right if you are facing the car park entrance. This path meanders along, with the road to your left. When the path opens out again nearer the road, you will see views over to Morven hill - a Corbett (mountains in Scotland between 2500 and 3000 feet high, with at least 500 feet of descent on all sides). Further along, the path leads into more of a wooded area and then directs you back towards the road again where you can start to see some houses and outbuildings.

This stretch is particularly striking in autumn, as expressed by Nan Shepherd in 'The Colours of Deeside',

"For the most flaming glory of autumn colour on Deeside, both in variety and close-packed intensity, one should go to those undulating heights from the Shooting Greens down to Potarch."[40]

Cross an access road, and continue straight on. Closer to the road again, a good bit further down the track there are some more houses on your left and over to the right the trees look particularly picturesque in later autumn with their orange-tinged tops. You will come to a boardwalk bridge over a burn, and as you come to the end of the boardwalk, I would encourage you to glance up to spot some very tall trees. There is another access road crossing, before continuing on – with the path veering slightly to the right. Turn right where there is a Deeside Way post and follow the path round.

The track leads you back around to a gate before crossing a road which can be busy. Once you are across, you will see a board welcoming you to Ballogie Estate, which also shows other suggested walking routes on the estate at Potarch. Follow the track round to the right, and as has been mentioned before, this section really is eye-catching in autumn with the most vibrant covering of golden and orange leaves.

BALLOGIE AND POTARCH

Follow along the obvious path, which has another wooden footbridge leading you into a car park, with a Green ahead of you and a number of picnic benches. You are now at Potarch and will see Potarch Café and Restaurant ahead of you.

Moving towards the lodge and you will see another Deeside Way post in front of it, signing to go right over the bridge.

18 Potarch & The Dinnie Stones The old hotel and inn is now the dog-friendly Potarch Café and Restaurant. The original inn dates from around 1814 when the bridge here at Potarch was completed, and considerably enlarged in 1897. The Dinnie Stanes (stones) - the famed training weights of Donald Dinnie - stand outside the café. These two stones with metal rings attached weigh a total of around 734lb (333kg). It is said that Dinnie's father used the stones as anchors while he was repairing the bridge and that on completion of the work his son carried them across the bridge and continued to use them as training weights.[41] He went on to become a renowned athlete and strongman.

{insta} @potarch   {fb} /potarch

As you cross the bridge, which was designed by the famous Scottish engineer, Thomas Telford, you are now passing back over the river Dee. Take care as it is quite narrow when there is traffic on it too. Head left once you are across the other side, passing a small car park with more interpretation panels about the area. You can read more about the bridge, the Dinnie Stanes, life on the river Dee and fishing, as well as learning about the upcoming village of Kincardine O'Neil and 'Jock Young's Loup' (to leap or jump in Scots), a local tale of a daring escape…

Beyond the board, head straight ahead past a bus stop and continue on the Deeside Way path. This is another access point for bus stops on both sides, at a busy section of road.

This part of the path heading towards Kincardine O'Neil is quite close to the road on your right, but is very scenic. On your left as you start this section there is a stile to the riverbank if you want to have a closer look at the Potarch Bridge from below as it looks impressive from this angle.

Potarch to Dess on the Deeside Way runs through the Kincardine Estate, which is explained on a board on the route, with more details about the land management of the estate, the castle, gardens and the kitchen enterprise of handcrafted baking and preserves, which are available to buy at the Kincardine O'Neil Village Store. There is also a link to their website: www.kincardinecastle.com.

Further along there is a quaint fishing hut over to your left, with an impressive backdrop, which always captures my attention. As you near the end of this flat section, there are a couple of inclines, the second being short but fairly steep and may be more challenging for some users. From here you are overlooking a couple of huts (which can be accessed from a stile at the foot of the incline).

It is very close to the A93 road at the top of this incline and it is also at a junction with a turnoff to Torphins. At this point with metal railings, there is a lovely view of the river looking back down to your left, and a fishing hut on the other bank. As you approach the village you will pass a market garden on your left, and then a Deeside Way post as you come into Kincardine O'Neil. Join up here with the high street, which has a number of charming old granite houses and cottages.

KINCARDINE O'NEIL

Kincardine O'Neil (known locally as 'Kinker') is the oldest village on Deeside. The railway line did not go through the village but ran from Banchory over to Torphins and Lumphanan before heading to Dess and then Aboyne.

The structure of the village has changed little since the 19th Century, with only a few houses having been built in the last century. Kincardine O'Neil is now designated a Conservation Area and several of the buildings are listed.[42]

Kincardine is believed to have derived from the Gaelic *'ceann na cearn'* meaning end of the hill or district, and in medieval times the land lay within the barony of Onele.[43]

🖲 **Kincardine O'Neil Village** The high street has a number of places to visit, including the Village Store which sells local produce and serves a great milky coffee. Ice cream and hot drinks are available at Love Laura Lane Cakes, The Old Smiddy currently houses Woodside Antiques & Collectables, and other local businesses include a gemstones shop called Treasures and the beautiful weaving studio and gallery - Arra Textiles. Hear from the owner of Arra textiles on page 110.

Bus stops in both directions are available on the high street, and public toilets operated by Aberdeenshire Council are located at the far end of the village.

One of the first landmarks you will come to is the ruined church of St Mary on your left. Kincardine O'Neil Old Parish Church is thought to have been built in the mid-14th Century AD. There is an interpretation board by Aberdeenshire Council just inside the gates with details of its long history and architectural features.

There is an optional additional walk just beyond the church, which adds an extra mile or so and takes you down to the river Dee. If you are continuing the Deeside Way, head to page 116.

PEOPLE OF THE DEESIDE WAY
Lucy MacDonald

Owner of Arra Textiles Studio in Kincardine O'Neil, Lucy MacDonald, shares how the Deeside Way weaves through her life, work, and leisure time...

"The Deeside Way (or as we still call it in our house, The Railway Line!) has been a part of my life for as long as I can remember. These days I use it to commute from Banchory to the studio in Kincardine O'Neil and to forage for dye plants on dog walks in the summer and autumn.

Studio visitors often ask for good spots to swim and paddleboard near the route, there's many but a couple of my favourites are under Potarch Bridge and the stretch of river by the Milton of Crathes."

{insta} @arratextiles

www.arratextiles.co.uk

Kincardine O'Neil Riverside Walk

0.9 MILES / 1.5 KM - EASY

This walk is from a leaflet produced by the Kincardine O'Neil Community Association in 2016.[44] A number of visitor and walking leaflets are available from the red telephone box outside the Old Smiddy on the high street in the village.

The walk takes around 30 minutes, taking you down to an old ford crossing of the Dee, which was one of the most important crossing points on the river. Here the ancient route linking Strathdon in the north with the Mearns in the south crossed at this point. The route, known as the Cairn O'Mount, intersected at this point - the hamlet surrounding it building up as use increased over the centuries.[45]

Take a left beyond the church down a track. Follow the track, and the river will draw you down, past vast fields and expansive skies overhead. This track was used by travellers for many centuries on their way to the ford across the Dee.[46]

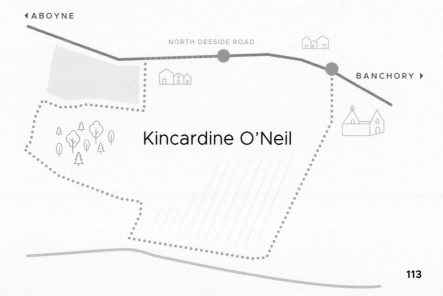

‹ABOYNE

NORTH DEESIDE ROAD

BANCHORY ›

Kincardine O'Neil

Turn right at the river and walk along the bank, the hill seen in the distance ahead being Morven again. After around 200 metres, you will reach the point of the ferry crossing, which was used until 1937 when a great spate swept the boat away. The river reached the same height as it did in 2015 during Storm Frank. The Ferryman's house can be seen across the other side of the river. This section of ground is relatively easy to walk on but is a little uneven in places, and there is also a bench to rest and enjoy the views.

Turn right up at the point opposite the Ferryman's house, towards the new build houses. You can follow this track back up to the main road, or lengthen the route slightly (an extra 400m) by heading left into 'Boat Woods' for an extra woodland loop, indicated by a Scottish Land and Estates sign. This track is a little uneven, and as you reach the point where the path turns to the right, it then narrows. Keep veering right and heading for the newer houses, walking alongside the back of the playpark. The path gets narrower and winding, but is still walkable. As you come to the end of the woodland path turn left and you can walk round the gates – which states it is Kincardine Estate land and you will come back onto the main road – the A93.

A sign for Deeside Log Cabins is along to the left, but turn right back along past some of the new houses for a short distance. At this point the Deeside Way continues up Pitmurchie Road by the Old Toll House, but if you missed out the village high street by taking the additional walk, I would recommend to visit that before continuing the route.

Kincardine O'Neil to Aboyne

6.1 MILES / 9.8 KM - MODERATE

KINCARDINE O'NEIL

ABOYNE

POINTS OF INTEREST:

- **20** Old Toll House
- **21** Bridge at Dess
- **22** Aboyne Loch
- **23** Aboyne Station
- **24** Spider on a Bicycle Cafe

Whether you are coming along from the high street or the additional walk direction, there is a Deeside Way sign on a lamppost directing you up Pitmurchie Road.

● **Old Toll House** The Deeside toll houses are an interesting feature. They were built as a means to collect tolls when the turnpike roads were developed, and the Kincardine O'Neil one,

which you pass as you head up Pitmurchie Road to continue the Deeside Way, has a semi-circular end onto the road with windows in order to watch the turnpike traffic.[47]

Walk up that road for around 275 metres, nearing the end of residential houses on both sides, where the road narrows straight on. Take the fork left at a signpost for the Deeside Way. This narrower path continues with houses to your right.

DESS

Keep going straight along this path. This takes you away from the road and is a lot quieter as fields appear and the route opens out more. It is spacious and picturesque and there are likely to be cattle in the fields and a variety of trees surrounding you. You will come to a gate with pedestrian and vehicle access, which you can go through and continue straight on.

Approaching a Deeside Way post, you take a left turn as directed. This part really opens out and rewards you with views for miles, vast skies, and horses in the nearby field to observe. Keep going straight on across two access tracks - the path inclines and winds its way ahead but is still very obvious. The pine trees give off a strong aroma in this section, especially if it has been raining. You will come to a couple of posts either side of the track, with a low bench to the left. There is a nice peaceful sense to this part, as you keep following the main path, straight on, which meanders slowly down the hill.

21 **Bridge at Dess** Coming to constructed steps on your right for dismounting (horses and cycles) there is a post with other walk route markers, one directing you towards the Dess waterfall (approximately 250m off route). For the Deeside Way you take a left and go over the wooden bridge, crossing the Dess Burn. There is another structure for re-mounting on the other side.

Once over the bridge, the path winds back uphill a little, coming out near a road where there is a metal gate and another Deeside Way post. This directs you to keep going to the left on the path you are currently on. Reaching a wooden fenced section with another incline, you come out at the road quite suddenly, which can be quite busy. Cross this road, seeing another Deeside Way post slightly to your left on the other side. Turn back round through the pedestrian gate and continue following the path. As you walk along, on your left are fields which usually have (enclosed) cattle.

Heading towards Aboyne

Continue on the path until you come to a set of gates providing access through farmland, followed shortly by more double gates as the track narrows, with the outline of Morven in the distance.

Further on, you can see where the old bank of the railway came through, and looking to the right you will see more sleeper posts as wooden fencing which lined the side of the rail track - a nice visual reminder of the route's rail heritage again. Heading up another slight incline, and approaching another gate, here you are coming onto the original railway line again. Mortlich, Aboyne's hill, comes into view at this point.

Another Deeside Way post indicates a left turn and the wide track has visible remnants of old ironwork. Some distance along at an access road, cross straight over, after which the track noticeably narrows. At the time of writing there is a very small diversion, visibly trodden, to rejoin the path. After this section you will come up to the sign below at Rosehill Croft.

This section is not officially part of the Deeside Way, but as stated on the notice, you can access it responsibly. The gates are a little trickier for this part, and you will then come out at the entrance to Lodge on the Loch, and the Aboyne Loch Golf Centre. Continue straight on as the path narrows, with the loch to your right.

Approaching a metal gate this time as you arrive at the entrance to Aboyne Caravan Park, which is quite near the road. Looking across for another metal gate, head through it to continue on this path away from the road.

22 **Aboyne Loch** There was a stop on the Deeside Railway Line before reaching Aboyne station – 'the curling stop'.[48] The platform can still be seen at the edge of the loch here, where curlers once stepped down from the train and onto the ice over the winter.

With the loch to your right, there is a warning notice of blue-green algae and not to go wild swimming. Continue on this path, and further along it will be the Aboyne Golf Course on your right as you approach the village.

ABOYNE

As you come into Aboyne, passing the petrol station on your left, carry straight on. Take the path along at the right towards the bridge archway, which you are going under, and you will come out onto the main road, the A93, heading right towards the village centre. Once you reach the shops and the main bus stops, there is a public toilet on your right.

Aboyne is a village of extreme temperatures and is regularly named the hottest place in the UK in summer, and one of the coldest in winter. With a spacious village green, and a number of cafés and shops, including John Troup butcher which has occupied the site since 1869, the Black Faced Sheep, general store Strachan's of Royal Deeside, and the newer Deeside Refill, to name a few - it is a nice place to spend some time along the route.

To resume on the Deeside Way, continue until you come to the Victory Hall on your right and you will see another marker post to resume the route – on page 126.

23 **Aboyne Station** The station architecture at Station Square is still quite easy to identify, although it is now transformed into business outlets. As Jane Geddes refers to it in her book, *Deeside and the Mearns – an illustrated architectural guide*, Aboyne Station is "*Undoubtedly the boldest style-statement on the Royal Deeside Line...Sprightly conical towers flank the ticket-office area*"[50]

24 **Spider on a Bicycle** Within the old station buildings in Aboyne is the café, Spider on a Bicycle. This was originally set up in 2016 and was sold to new owners, under the same name, in 2022. It also features in the *Scottish Independent Coffee Guide* (5th edition). Make sure you look up when you are inside to take in the architectural features of the ceiling as the setting really does add to the experience. The café offers speciality coffee, chai and a range of cakes, bakes and as they describe it – 'simple food with flavours'. Cosy up at the woodburning stove in the colder months in this dog friendly space with bike racks outside and a warm welcome inside. **www.spideronabicycle.co.uk**

{insta} @spideronabicycle

The next section from Aboyne to Ballater lends itself well to cycling, and Aboyne is the base for eguide Scotland bike hire and guiding. Having had a guided e-bike trip with them on the route, I can recommend the experience.

PEOPLE OF THE DEESIDE WAY
Tony Yule

Owner of eguide Scotland, Tony Yule, is a qualified mountain bike guide - an expert at planning mountain bike adventures showcasing the best trails and scenery in Scotland...including the Deeside Way.

"For eguide Scotland the Deeside Way is both the journey and the destination. The ever-changing landscape and the ease at which the 'Way' enables all to access and enjoy it is truly special."

{insta} @eguidescotland   **www.eguidescotland.com**

Aboyne to Ballater

ABOYNE

DINNET

BALLATER

Aboyne to Ballater

11 MILES / 17.7KM - MODERATE

This section of the Deeside Way follows the route of the old railway line which is evident in a number of sites along the path. The Deeside Gliding Club airfield is beyond the village of Aboyne, and this section transitions into the 'Highlands' and the Cairngorms National Park, marked with boundary stones. Dinnet Station and platform are still in situ, and are opposite the starting point for the additional Loch Kinord circular walk. Cambus O'May also has a rich rail heritage, a distinctive suspension bridge, and a cheese dairy and café. Tullich is the site of a restored historic Kirkyard and Pictish Stones, and the Old Royal Station in the Victorian village of Ballater is the official end of the Deeside Way route.

Aboyne to Dinnet

4.5 MILES / 7.3 KM - MODERATE

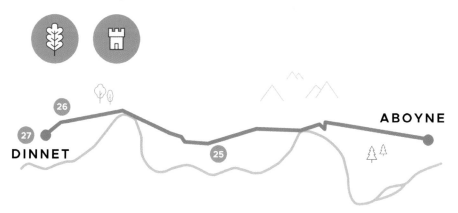

This section of the walk starts beside The Aboyne & Glen Tanar Memorial Hall (The Victory Hall). If you are there in late July/early August, you may be lucky enough to catch the annual Artaboyne

exhibition which takes place at this venue. The Aboyne Highland Games take place on the first Saturday of August on the village green.

There is a Deeside Way post to the left of the building and a post a short distance after which indicates going straight on - although the path slightly veers to the left. Further along you will pass under a road archway, this is a nice wooded section with a clear path. After another stretch you come to the Tarland Road crossing (also the beginning point of the Tarland Way route - continue across where you will see another post.
www.tarland.org.uk/the-tarland-way

POINTS OF INTEREST:
25 Deeside Gliding Club
26 Boundary Stone & Cairngorms National Park
27 Dinnet Old Station

A couple of Deeside Way posts will continue directing you straight on until you arrive at the end of a section at an access track, and this time you will see a post indicating a left turn. Moving along the track, you will see you are approaching the A93, but just before you reach the main road there is another post diverting you to turn right, entering more of a wooded section again.

This path winds round to the right initially and then to the left. At the back of this area are old railway sleepers which edged the fencing for the tracks. You can glimpse the road over to your left, once again surrounded by silver birch as you approach the A93. Traffic can be fast here and visibility can vary, so take care crossing at this point as you head straight over. There is another post to follow the track on the opposite side, now back on the side closer to the river Dee, which you can see down the bank on the left.

Deeside Way posts will direct you to keep going straight on, walking parallel to the main road on your right for much of this section.

25 **Deeside Gliding Club** Deeside Gliding Club is renowned for having the best soaring conditions in the UK. It is quite a sight to see a glider take off above you as you follow the Deeside Way route, and there are a number of picnic benches and interpretation boards encouraging you to dwell while passing the airfield. I imagine the views from above are pretty spectacular. **www.deesideglidingclub.co.uk**

Another Deeside Way post is at the other end of the car park, directing you straight on. You will cross the vehicle access track to the airfield, and beyond that are scenic open views, and fields to your left. The path is lined with bracken and there are poignant remains of the railway at points on the right.

After a stretch you will see the river again in the distance if you look back down to the left, before coming to another access track with a post, continuing straight on. Moving on along the old rail line, you will cross more access tracks as you pass by a few houses, heading towards the village of Dinnet – with a number of Deeside Way posts directing you straight on.

26 **Boundary Stones** The boundary stones signal that you are now entering the Cairngorms National Park and 'the Highlands'. One signals the point at which the route crosses into the Cairngorms National Park, and the other is the Highland Boundary Stone, a large block of granite which was erected by the Deeside Field Club in 1980 – saying that *'You are now in the Highlands'*. On the Deeside Way this is a little further on from a wooden footbridge and is visible from the track depending on the time of year, owing to the tree coverage.

DINNET

There is a beautiful birch wood on your left as you approach Dinnet and come into the village around the back of the Dinnet Garage.

㉗ Dinnet Old Station Fragments of the railway are evident here with sections of the old platform, ironworks and the boundary lines of the tracks edged with railway sleeper posts. You really get a sense of the old station setting here, and although nature has reclaimed much of it, the building is still in its original location. It is now the Dinnet Estate office.

Approaching a crossroads with another Deeside Way post, take care crossing this road as it can be a busy connection to the South Deeside Road with a bridge over the river. Head straight across the road and continue on the marked Deeside Way trail. There is an option to go on an additional walk and head to your right a small distance along - crossing the A93 main road over to the car park area to start the walk. This will give you the chance to explore Loch Kinord and the Burn O'Vat, which are part of the Muir of Dinnet National Nature Reserve (NNR), managed by NatureScot. Dinnet also offers bus stops in both directions at this point.

If you are continuing on the Deeside Way route, head to page 146.

Loch Kinord & Burn O'Vat/ Muir of Dinnet NNR

4.5 MILES / 7.3 KM - STRENUOUS

Allow 2.5-3 hours for this walk, which enters a mixed woodland of pine and birch, circumnavigating Loch Kinord, part of the Muir of Dinnet National Nature Reserve (NNR). There is much to see, from abundant wildlife to many sites of historic interest, including Castle Island, the Celtic Cross, and the chapel at Meikle Kinord on the south side of the loch. A visit to the Burn O'Vat is also recommended to see this geological wonder.

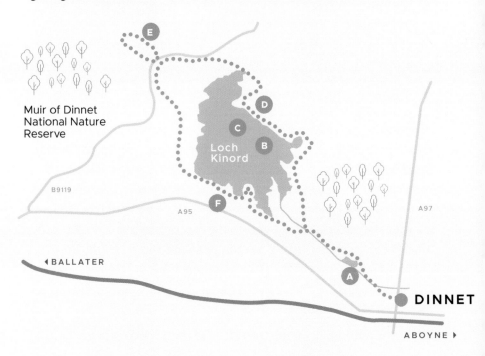

POINTS OF INTEREST:

- (A) Viewing Platform over Clarack Loch
- (B) Crannog Island
- (C) Castle Island
- (D) Celtic Cross
- (E) Visitor Centre & The Vat Trail
- (F) Meikle Kinord Chapel

From the back of the car park, follow the sign for the Loch Kinord circular walk. You will see a track to start the walk, with lodges to your left and a series of posts with orange arrow markers to follow. Pass a hut on your left (a hide) and a bench and then come round to a small bridge over a burn, with another post and arrowed sign signalling to go to the left.

Ⓐ Viewing Platform Over Clarack Loch

You will arrive at Clarack Loch and see the wooden viewing platform, a lovely spot to pause and appreciate the surroundings.

The path is quite rocky for part of this section, especially with tree roots, so take extra care with your footing. This section can be alive with birdsong and I have often heard woodpeckers in this part. Following the path near the pylons, you will come up to two gates, crossing an access track and continuing straight on. Head through another couple of open gate posts, and there will be a Muir of Dinnet marker sign on your right. As this is a circular route, you will return to this section, but for now, head straight up on the right.

 Parkin's Moss Trail

 Little Ord Trail

 Loch Kinord Trail

Follow the path and come to a sign encouraging you to look out for geese roosting on the lochs over the autumn and winter. Continue on the well-trodden track with fields opening up on your right, following posts with a duck symbol (The Loch Kinord Trail) and another notice to look out for otters fishing in the loch – with dawn and dusk being suggested as the best times. Winding down the path with Loch Kinord coming into view, the scale of it always seems impressive and the islands definitely draw interest. There are interpretation panels which explain their history.

B Crannog Island

A man-made island built about 2,500 years ago. The board gives further information on log boats and crannog building, and explains that an enormous log boat was discovered in 1875 and was nicknamed the 'Royal Yacht'. It was a metre wide and 9.2 metres long, slightly longer than a London bus.[51]

C Castle Island

It is fascinating that there was once a castle on the next island you can see across the loch, for 600 years, which had a causeway. Another interpretation panel illustrates this royal retreat which was used as a power base by Scotland's nobles, kings and queens, and a retreat for hunting game in the local oak forests. The panel also shares other snippets on wolves, lilies and legends.[52]

Continue on the well signed and obvious path which has a bit of an incline as you approach the Celtic Cross.

D Celtic Cross (The Kinord Cross)

Another interpretation board explains more about the religious history of the area, the design on the cross, and the various locations it has had over the years. Carved over 1,000 years ago, the Pictish Cross overlooks the loch once again.

Head straight on until you come to another post and turn left to continue along the track. This next part of the path is a bit more undulating, winding through beautiful birch forest, and passing another interpretation panel about how the landscape was shaped by ice. Arriving at a marker stone for the nature reserve, it is also a commemorative plaque marking the Silver Jubilee for Her Majesty Queen Elizabeth II in September 1977.

Keep veering right on the path at this point. You will come to a road with the Burn O'Vat Visitor Centre and car park on the opposite side, so take care crossing over.

E Burn O'Vat Visitor Centre & The Vat Trail

The visitor centre building itself is not always open but there are accessible picnic benches, bike racks, toilets and a car park. The Vat Trail starts behind the toilets, and it is a nice clear path along to the waterfall, signed straight on as you come to a post with a path also to the right.

Directing you straight ahead to the waterfall, a short distance along you will reach the entrance to the rocky bowl of the Burn O'Vat. This striking geological wonder of pink granite, which was formed by a river flowing underneath the glaciers that covered the land about 20,000 years ago,[53] was once thought to be the hiding place of Rob Roy MacGregor. It was likely another well known outlaw, Gilderoy, who used it.[54] Take care and make sure you have waterproof boots on for heading into the Vat itself. It an adventurous experience and quite an awe-inspiring sight.

Once out of the Vat, head back along the path for a short distance and turn left along the track at the post signed for the Vat Trail. This section is a steeper incline, which rewards as you head to a beautiful viewpoint up ahead. You will pass some rocks with words carved in them such as 'ICE', before reaching the viewpoint itself, a wooden structure with intricate carvings interpreting the surroundings, including the wildlife, the Cross and the silver birch. The path meanders back down to the car park from here. Cross back over the road to restart the circular Loch Kinord Trail (the duck symbol) again, turning right.

This is a pleasant path back, crossing a wooden bridge, and heading straight on at a minor crossroads in the track, edged with a charming drystane dyke. Continue following the duck symbols on the posts, through more silver birch woods. Approaching the loch again, the path veers to the left, and you will spot an old chapel building.

F Meikle Kinord Chapel

According to Canmore, this private chapel was built around 1880, and was converted into a museum in 1912 to house the oak canoes found in the area, but is now used only as a hay-store. It may have been built on the site of a much earlier chapel which served the castle on the island in the loch.[55]

You will keep walking near to the loch on your left, with fields to your right. You can see over to the A93 road again at this point too, which is more obvious when a bus goes past. The path is quite narrow but this section seems to lead back to the bridge more quickly, back to the Muir of Dinnet sign. Retrace your steps back to the car park following the orange arrows, along the path near the pylons, and past the viewing platform. When arriving back to the car park, cross the road at the exit near the pay and display machine, heading back onto the Deeside Way path signed for Cambus O'May to the right.

Dinnet to Ballater

6.5 MILES / 10.4 KM - MODERATE

DINNET

BALLATER

POINTS OF INTEREST:

- **28** Cambus O'May Bridge
- **29** Cambus O'May Cheese Company
- **30** Fingerpost to 'The Needle'
- **31** Tullich Kirkyard
- **32** Ballater Station

Back on the Deeside Way, this is a long stretch of old railway line, which means you are heading in a straight line for what feels like quite a long way. The pine trees appear to have grown taller and the woods feel denser and more shaded in this section, which can make it even cooler in the winter months. The road is quite close on your right but you will deviate away from it as you go on. The surroundings here are peaceful and feel a little mysterious, with a chance of spotting deer. It might seem like you are not making much progress on this part as you can see so far into the distance, but you are - keep going!

Due to this long linear track, this would be a good section for cycling. The path is clear and direct - it is essentially straight on with a few access roads to cross, one of which has a sign signalling a road crossing. There are also Deeside Way posts dotted along. If you are walking, you may be more likely to notice the remnants of the rail track, and as it tends to be a quiet and calm section, the bird song can be a nice soundtrack as you ramble.

This section from Dinnet can feel a little repetitive at times without seeing the broader views as much, but the birch forests on both sides of the path are enchanting, especially in the autumn with the varied rich ochre tones. Walking this path on a bright day in October, the sun bounces off the silver birch bark and illuminates the golden leaves. As you near Cambus O'May, the views do slowly start to open up again, especially on the right as you look over to Muir of Dinnet NNR and Culbean Hill, and it feels lighter and more expansive again.

Coming to a footbridge to cross over an access road, you continue straight on. Slightly further on in this section there is often a strong scent of the pine trees, especially enhanced after any rain. There is another Deeside Way post indicating to go straight on, and the views open up more to the left, becoming more diverse as you are near the river again at this point - a welcome sight.

CAMBUS O'MAY

The name Cambus O'May comes from the Gaelic and means 'Crook in the Plain', referring to the tight bend in the river Dee near the old station. You may spot a different type of sign directing forward to Ballater and back to Dinnet as you near the old Cambus O'May Station, which closed to passengers in 1966 and is now a private residence.

28 **Cambus O'May Bridge** There has been a suspension bridge here from 1905, the previous one spanning the railway line. The current bridge, which is a Grade B listed structure, was built in 1988 but became badly damaged in the severe flood of the river in 2015. Following major repair works, it re-opened in 2021.

At the bridge there is picnic bench, a scenic stopping place. The quaint house on the right is called *'Cutaway Cottage'*, an old ferry inn. It is named so due to alterations on the gable end of the building when the railway track was being built, to ensure sufficient clearance.

There is another post along the narrower track beyond the cottage indicating to go round to the right, and continuing on the main path which is nearer to the road again. As you approach the hamlet you will see a road sign for the Cambus O'May forest trails car park 300 yards along. Houses emerge on the right, and there are lovely views of the river down to the left. You will come to the first Deeside Way post in a while, signalling to continue straight on, and also mentioning the Cambus O'May circular route. The hamlet has bus stops in either direction, and access to the forest trails.

29 Cambus O'May Cheese Co. - Creamery & Milk Hoose Café

The Deeside Way leads directly to the Cambus O'May Cheese Co., a family business with an interesting story of its cheesemaking history – which you can read on interpretation panels along the side of the creamery. You can also buy produce in the Milk Hoose café, as well as coffees, cakes, scones and a selection of cheese-based plates and toasties. There is spacious outdoor seating, surrounded by birch. The café also serves Deeside Mineral Water from the nearby Pannanich Wells.

{insta} @themilkhoose {fb} /cambuscheese

Leaving the Cambus O'May cheese company, there are steps back up onto the Deeside Way with bike racks and a cheese press.

Opposite is also a café and bakery called Courie Courie (a Scots word meaning to nestle or snuggle), which specialises in artisan sourdough and is a friendly wholefood café. Look out for their produce appearing at many of the Deeside Farmers' Markets as well as suppling local businesses.

TULLICH

A short distance along the Deeside Way you will see a road sign signalling that you are coming into the village bounds of Tullich, as you follow the path alongside the road. This is also the first sighting of Lochnagar, 'Deeside's Mountain' and an impressive Munro (a mountain in Scotland with a height over 3,000 feet (914.4 m)) described by the poet Lord Byron, who spent his formative years in Aberdeen, as *'Dark Lochnagar'*.[57]

This section is quite close to the road, but it really opens out with the farmland to the left, and seeing the impressive hills in the distance makes it feel more epic.

30 **Fingerpost to the 'The Needle'** This marker details a monument on top of the hillock accessed through a gate to your left if you are facing ahead on the path towards Ballater. It commemorates William Farquharson, Laird of Monaltrie - who is credited with developing the village of Ballater. He and his wife had no children, so the lands went to their cousins at Invercauld when they died. His wife Margaret chose this hillock, with its views of Lochnagar, to erect an impressive monument to him. It is not far to walk up to the marker, but beware that the field may be in use for cattle grazing.[58]

It feels like you have shifted into a slightly different type of environment here. I think this is one of the highlights of the whole walk, especially on a sunny day.

As James Coutts wrote in *Dictionary of Deeside*,

"The greater mountains do not, however, force themselves much on the view till Ballater is neared, great precipices and spots of snow visible late in summer marking out the 'Caledonian Alps' as Byron called them."[59]

Coming up to the fishery across the road on the right, there is an access path to cross, and a Deeside Way marker directing you straight on. The scenery and vast views towards the hills on this section make it a sight appreciated by many.

"Heading West from Dinnet towards Ballater, Tullich comes into view and is always a special place for me. On a clear day heading into the Summer, the 15th century Kirk looks nestled into the landscape surrounded with the most beautiful trees that are lush and green, set against the magnificent Lochnagar in the distance. It is the one view that always reminds me how lucky I feel to call this place home."

Cheryl Roberts, Tullich Kirkyard Restoration Project Manager. Cheryl is also a Banchory resident and features on page 99.

31 **Tullich Kirkyard and Pictish Stones** Tullich Kirk (Church) is a nationally important Scheduled Monument which has undergone a sensitive repair and consolidation led by Aberdeenshire Council with support from the North East Preservation Trust (NESPT). You can access the Kirkyard from a section on the right - a panel that refers to the Tullich carved stone, then go through three access gates, being careful of cattle. Follow round to the right past the edge of the wall and you'll come to the display case for some of the Pictish stones that were found in the Kirk. There is also an interpretation panel in the churchyard giving further history and context to Tullich Church.

Back on the Deeside Way, there are several modern interpretation installations, telling of the history of the community at Tullich, the carved stones, and the history of the church site itself. Continue straight on at another access track, following the clear path, and taking in the spacious rural surroundings of farmland and cattle.

Crossing a couple of footbridges, over to your right will be the *'Pass of Ballater'* route to Braemar, as you approach the main road (A93) crossing.

There is a warning sign again asking cyclists and horse riders to dismount. Visibility is poor round a corner here and the cars are usually going fast so take extra care. Head straight on to the other side, then over a small footbridge. The A93 traffic is now over to your left, and you are following the old rail track route into Ballater. If you glance back behind you over to the trees in the distance, you can see Tullich Lodge nestled into the hills on the left.

BALLATER

Following along on the path, you will start to see more houses around you on the left as you approach the edge of Ballater village. Now in the residential part of Ballater, there are several Deeside Way signs directing you to go straight on. Coming into the station, you approach it from the back, with the platform on your left-hand side. Come up the steps on the left and out at The Old Royal Station, as mentioned below, the official end of the walk.

32 **Ballater Station** The Old Royal Station re-opened in the summer of 2018 as the previous station was destroyed by a fire in 2015. This current station has been painted in line with the palette that was there at the time the station was in operation, and it now houses a VisitScotland information centre, a restaurant and tearoom run by The Prince's Foundation, and a public library - as well as the Royal waiting room and carriage.

This was the final stop for passengers on the Deeside Railway Line, as it is widely said that Queen Victoria did not want the train passing by Balmoral Castle, or as she was quoted as saying she wished *"the upper part of the Dee Valley to be preserved as a natural Highland Region."*[60]

Ballater is a Victorian village, which grew in popularity due to the believed curative powers of the waters of the nearby Panninach Wells. The village is relatively modern dating from around 1798 and has many Royal connections. H M Sheridan butcher, which began trading in 1963, and many other shops in the town have been granted Royal Warrants.

Just beside the station is another long-established Ballater business - Dee Valley Confectioners. From 1965 it has specialised in traditional handmade sweets, and 'Soor Plooms' are what Kylie Minogue apparently bought when she visited the shop in 2016, which made it into the press.

Ballater is also the birthplace of Sir Patrick Geddes, renowned for his innovative thinking in the fields of urban planning and sociology, and for coining the term 'think global, act local'. There is a street named Sir Patrick Geddes Way in the village.

Today, Ballater is a very popular visitor destination, offering a number of quality coffee shops, cycling specialist companies, including Cyclehighlands which has had its base there since 2004 and bookshops, namely A.B.Yule and the predominately rare and out of print bookshop, Deeside Books. It is also an access point with a bus terminus outside the Co-op. A popular farmers' market runs on the fourth Saturday of the month, April to November, and a number of events and festivals run in Ballater throughout the year. www.visitballater.com

Polhollick Bridge

4.8 MILES / 7.7 KM - MODERATE

This suggested walk takes around 3 hours there and back. It partially follows the section of the Deeside Line which was built as part of the original plans for the railway. It was used for goods transport only and went as far as the Bridge of Gairn.

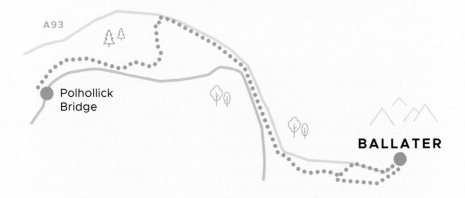

Standing with the station on your right, go straight on and cross the main road (A93 - Braemar Road) and continue until you see a right turn into Queens Road, which is noticeably wide in its regal stature, and houses striking granite buildings with charming names. It is also home to the Victoria Barracks of the 51 Infantry Brigade, marked by the white metal railings at the far end of this street.

At the end of Queens Road, beyond the barracks, turn slightly to the right onto Invercauld Road, then left, signed for Dandarroch Road. The posts to follow for this route initially are signed for the Seven Bridges Walk – the blue arrow posts. Following straight on across a road (Braemar Place) you will see a road sign on your left called 'Old Line Road', giving a clue that you are in the right place for this walk. Beyond a number of houses, you will then come to a green

waymarker. Continue to follow the directions for the Seven Bridges Walk, with the blue arrows.

This is a lovely part where you are following the old railway line that was built along this section. With the river Dee to your left, and depending on the time of year, the shallow water here can have an almost translucent quality, which has tones of aqua colours flowing through it.

Crossing a small wooden bridge over a ravine, this is known as 'Postie's Leap' – so called apparently after a lovelorn postman was jilted on the eve of his wedding, and walked along the 'Auld (Old) Line', where he jumped to his death at this point.[61] You will see on the other side of the river is a log cabin, and there are benches along here providing the chance to sit and enjoy these spectacular views. You will also see an embankment wall on your right from the rail infrastructure.

Continue on as you move away from the river with fields coming into view on your left. Another post with blue markers signals you to curve to the right and follow that path along until you come up to the

Bridge of Gairn. This is the third bridge that was built over the Gairn, erected in 1855.

There is another green waymarker at this point and you take the sloped path down to your left as signed for the Seven Bridges Walk (via the river). There is also a blue arrow post and a sign on the building on the left cautioning of horses. Pass around the back of a farmyard and stables until you see another post indicating a right turn over a small wooden bridge and follow the path round to the left, through a gate.

As you cross the bridge there is a nice view over to your right of the Bridge of Gairn. The Waters of Gairn flow very closely on your left as you walk along this section. There are more posts with blue arrows to keep you on track for this section, which has picturesque open views.

There is a small water crossing with some stepping stones and markers to take you closer towards the Dee again, with its stony beach edging the river. This is a good spot for a picnic or drink by the water, and if you are lucky you might see a red kite flying overhead – its distinctive deeply forked tail easier to identify than some. There were some trees down in this section in early 2022, but the route is passable with care.

The edge of Polhollick Bridge will slowly come into view, as you continue to follow the blue arrows. It's bright white metal structure interrupting the green, brown and blue shades of the surrounding landscape, making it quite striking coming into view from this perspective. Coming up to a gate, there is another set of green waymarker signs. Take a left here signed for Ballater (via the Seven Bridges Walk) and my recommendation here is essentially to head to the bridge - and over it if you like - then to return, but you can of course continue on this blue arrowed route for another 3 miles at this stage round to the Bridge of Muick, past the Mackenzie Memorial and back over the bridge at the other end of Ballater village.

THIS BRIDGE
WAS PRESENTED
TO THE PUBLIC BY
Mr ALEXANDER GORDON
SOUTHWOOD
HILDENBOROUGH KENT
ERECTED 1892

The hut to the left of the bridge, and one you passed under the Bridge of Gairn, are SEPA monitoring stations. As the plaque states, the suspension bridge was presented to the public by Mr Alexander Gordon of Kent, an exile of Ballater, and built in 1892. There is a safety notice advising of a maximum of four people on the bridge at any one time. Before the bridge, there had previously been a ferry at Polhollick, crossing a well-known angling pool known as the 'Boat Pool'. The boathouse is still there today as a private dwelling.[62]

For the return journey, retrace your steps and follow the blue trails back the same way you came until you come back onto Invercauld Road, where the green signs started. Take a left this time down towards Braemar Road, where there is an Auld Kirk at the end of the road with a statue to commemorate the Diamond Jubilee of Queen Victoria's reign, and the fiftieth year of her residence at Balmoral – in 1898. Take a right signed for Station Square, and you will return back to Ballater Station, passing a gallery on route.

FURTHER ALONG THE ROAD...

Ballater to Braemar

Further along the road...

Heading towards Braemar

Ballater to Braemar is 17 miles. There is currently no connecting track, but it is hoped this will be part of future development plans. Crathie and Braemar have many points of interest, and it made sense to also include them in this book as the villages are accessible by bus from Ballater - see page 20 for transport information.

CRATHIE

Crathie is a natural stopping place on the road between Ballater and Braemar with further Royal connections, and you can get there by road along the A93. Balmoral Castle and Estate is based at Crathie, as is Crathie Church, and the village also hosts two great cafés - The Highlanders Bakehouse and Tarmachan Café.

POINTS OF INTEREST:

- 33 Tarmachan Café
- 34 The Highlanders Bakehouse
- 35 Balmoral Castle & Estate

33 **Tarmachan Café** As you approach Crathie, Tarmachan Café is just off the main road on the right. The setting is quite unique as the building was designed by Moxon Architects, whose studio sits behind the cafe. RIBA Journal describes the building: *"nestled into the curve of an old quarry, the strong concrete lines of its chimneys stand proud amidst the silver birch, rowan, juniper and alder. A black colonnade protects café tables from the weather."* [63]

Serving artisan bakes and speciality coffee, with the Cairngorms surrounding it, this dog friendly venue is definitely recommended to visit. Look out for ad hoc events they also host, such as supper clubs. **www.tarmachancafe.com**

{insta} @tarmachan_cafe

34 **The Highlanders Bakehouse** The Highlanders Bakehouse is a shop, bakery and café a little further along on the right, just back from the main road and next to the primary school. The Bakehouse serves quality coffee and sells a range of appetising foods, including breads and baked goods. A favourite is the butteries – a north east 'delicacy' and a great snack to keep you going on outdoor pursuits - definitely worth a try. You may spot their produce on offer at farmers' markets along Deeside too.

The Bakehouse is very dog friendly, with dog beds, water bowls and dog treats awaiting your adventure companions.

{insta} @thehighlandersbakehouse

35 **Balmoral Castle & Estate** Balmoral Castle & Estate is a popular attraction with visitors coming from far and wide to visit the majesty of the summer residence of the Royal Family. Owned by the family since the 19th century, and described by Queen Victoria as *'my dear paradise in the Highlands'*. The 'Balmoral Cairns Walk' on the estate is also popular and features Scotland's best known pyramid. **www.balmoralcastle.com**

BRAEMAR

Braemar is not part of the Deeside Way at the moment, although there have long been plans mentioning this intention, so it may link up one day. The village gets its name from the Gaelic *'braigh Mhàrr'* - the upland of Mar.

POINTS OF INTEREST:

- **36** Braemar Castle
- **37** Great North of Scotland Railway Building
- **38** The Bothy Braemar
- **39** Kindrochit Castle
- **40** Braemar Highland Games Centre

The village of Braemar is popular with outdoor enthusiasts year-round, including skiing in the winter at the nearby Glenshee Ski Centre. It is another place that is rich in history, with Jacobite tales and two castles - one community run, and one a ruined fortification with visitor interpretation.

36 **Braemar Castle** Braemar Castle dates back to 1628 when it was built by the 2nd Earl of Mar and has a rich history linked to the Jacobite uprisings. A fascinating place to visit offering tours and events, it has been operated by the local community since 2007. At the time of writing, it is undergoing a restoration project called 'Raising the Standard' with the aim to re-open in July 2023. **www.braemarcastle.co.uk**

There have been artistic installations outside Braemar Castle for a number of years and prior to its temporary closure, the neon installation reassuring that *'Everything is going to be alright'* was striking and emotive, and a photographer's dream. The installation was by Turner Prize-winning artist Martin Creed.

37 **Great North of Scotland Railway Building** Within the village behind the Invercauld Arms hotel is a very unique building which was the Braemar depot of the Great North of Scotland Railway. Built in 1904 for linking motor services between the village and the railway terminus at Ballater, the depot is the oldest purpose-built bus depot in Scotland[65], and is now private residences.

Braemar was originally two villages, separated by the Clunie Water - Castleton, the older of the two on the east bank, and Auchindryne on the opposite bank. The bridge connecting these two settlements was built in 1863.

Author Robert Louis Stevenson (RLS), on holiday in Braemar in 1881 wrote a letter to a friend that *"the Queen knows a thing or two – she worked out the finest habitable spot in Britain."*[64] During that same summer in the village, he wrote Treasure Island. There is a plaque above the door on the residence he stayed in, celebrating this connection.

38 **The Bothy Braemar** The Bothy Braemar is a favourite place to go for a coffee and scone post-walk, with the building also connected to the outdoor shop, Braemar Mountain Sports. It is licensed, dog friendly and offers incredible views over the river Clunie. *{insta} @bothy_braemar*

Braemar has a selection of small independent shops, some which have been there for decades. The village has many food outlets including a chocolatier, a pâtissière, and a family-owned butcher as well as an array of craftsmen, compromised of horn carvers, sporran makers and

woodworkers. For an up-to-date glimpse into what Braemar offers, visit: www.braemarscotland.co.uk

A striking building in the heart of the village, the Fife Arms underwent an extensive renovation and re-opened in late 2018. It is now a 5-star boutique hotel *(pictured below)*. The architects that worked on the building are Moxon Architects, who are behind Tarmachan Café - mentioned in the Crathie section of the book on page 166. There has been substantial investment in the village in recent years and the Invercauld Hotel is also undergoing renovation at the time of writing.

39 Kindrochit Castle The ruined fortification of Kindrochit Castle is situated to the right of the public car park in Braemar and behind Farquharson's Bar and Kitchen. Believed to have been built in the late 1300s, this Scheduled Monument was re-opened in 2015 following remedial works, access improvements and new interpretation. There are a number of interpretation boards on site now which further tell the story of the castle through the centuries.

40 **Highland Games Centre** Celebrating Braemar's world-famous Highland Games - with Royal attendance - is the new Highland Games Centre in the village. Discover the 200-year history and traditions of the world-famous Braemar Gathering. The centre houses a café, shop, and also offers guided tours.
www.highlandgamescentre.org

Queen's Drive Circular

2.5 MILES / 4 KM - MODERATE

This 1-1.5 hour circular route initially follows alongside Clunie Water, also edging the beautiful setting of Braemar Golf Club - the highest golf club above sea level in the UK. It then picks up the track of the Queen's Drive, a carriage drive that reputed to be one of Queen Victoria's favourites. This has a steeper descent back through the woods to Braemar. There is also the option to return to the village more directly via the A93 Glenshee Road.

This walk starts from the War Memorial at the corner of Cluniebank Road/Invercauld Road and heads South towards the golf course. Take care walking on the road, which follows alongside Clunie Water. There are some interesting houses to pass, and you may even notice a sign along the way warning of '*Squirrels Crossing*'.

Head along this road until you come to a bench and a green bridge on the left. Cross this bridge, which is the Royal Highland Bridge, then go round to the right, over a small footbridge and along a grassy fence-lined path. You are now on the other side of the Clunie Water with views over the river and Morrone Birkwood beyond to your right.

The path then meanders round to the left, still following the route of the water and with the golf course coming into view on your right - a very impressive place for a round. Keep following the path as you pass through the first gate, enjoying the open views back to the village and the surrounding hills, until you get to a second gate, shortly before you reach the A93 road.

Crossing the road, you will see ahead of you the hills covered in beautiful birch woodland. You could take a left to return to the village more directly along Glenshee Road, passing the caravan park, the snow gates (which shut if this road is impassable), the Braemar Hostel and a number of other businesses and accommodation providers. The suggested route continues for another mile and a half, heading to the right initially and signed for the Queen's Drive and Lion's Face route.

This wider track then veers back to the left and gains height, giving sweeping views through the characterful forest, and over to the snow capped hills, depending on the time of year. When you reach a green footpath sign marked for Braemar 'Village Centre', take this turn to the left.

The path now descends through the woods, running alongside a wall and then passing through a gap in it. When it meets a bench keep left, then continue ahead at further junctions as the route continues to descend. At the bottom of the woods there is a signpost where other walking routes join it from the right. Continue straight on here to leave the woods through a gate, veering slightly to the right as you come onto this road. Keep straight to reach St. Margaret's - a performance, arts and heritage venue - and back to the centre of the village.

Further beyond the road...

Beyond the village of Braemar lies the Linn of Dee, which is part of the National Trust for Scotland managed Mar Lodge Estate. This is the gateway to the source of the Dee, to the Munros of the Eastern Cairngorm mountains - *'gateway to some of the finest mountain country in Scotland'*[66] – also Nan Shepherd's stomping ground, joy and inspiration. She reflects on page one of *The Living Mountain*...

"However often I walk on them, these hills hold astonishment for me. There is no getting accustomed to them."[67]

Although there is currently no access to the Linn of Dee by public transport, it is well worth a visit if time and circumstances allow.

AFTERWORD

Re-walking the Deeside Way to share it with others has made me view it through new eyes yet again. It has also fed my curiosity to learn more about the tree species and the wider flora and fauna along the route as well as the place names. Discovering so many place names are from the Gaelic language was a bit of a surprise with the north east being more associated with Doric. Daniel MacCannel's book *Lost Deeside* goes into depth about the *'Lost Language of Deeside'* and it's Gaelic origins.

I have found such joy in getting reacquainted with the route for this purpose, and will continue my research more each time I go on the path. Nan Shepherd's quote at the beginning of this book is so apt for both places and people, in that *'knowing another is endless'*.

The walks specifically for the book were done after work, at lunchtimes, over weekends and on days off. One of the things I love about the route is that it is accessible to venture on and off regularly, doing different sections at varying times, or it can also be a planned multi-day adventure.

In the four years since I travelled it all in one weekend, and even since I started this book, some areas of the walk have changed, even in subtle ways. Printing a publication is bound to date, but I also think there is still a place for printed literature, especially as a companion guide. This is a snapshot of the Deeside Way in 2021/2022.

Storm Arwen and a number of other winter storms happened during the time of writing, which had a substantial impact on the north east. Be aware you may still see evidence of this, and continuing forestry operations.

Whichever way you experience the route, I hope you will see it as more than a walk, a cycle, a run or any other mode of travel you choose. Deeside really is a special place with its own unique charm - a region with vast heritage, depth and majestic beauty.

Fenton Wyness writes in a chapter called *'The valley's recorders'* from his 1968 book, *'Royal Valley - The Story of the Aberdeenshire Dee'*:

"The recording of Deeside goes on for always there are interesting discoveries to be made, fresh pieces of history to be linked with what is already known, new methods used for scientific investigations, modern forms of expression employed by the artists or a novel approach made by photographers."[68]

I look forward to the continued interpretations and recordings of Deeside.

ACKNOWLEDGEMENTS

With thanks to Charlene Cheesman of Bosk Creative, for helping to bring this book to life as I had always hoped and envisioned. Your ideas, attention to detail, photography skills and good company have been such a wonderful addition to working on the project. The visuals are also thanks to Elin Beattie's atmospheric photography, and her endless patience and positivity on our enjoyable days out capturing Deeside.

Thanks go to Crawford Paris for the inspiration behind the idea, and to David Oswald at Aberdeen City Libraries, Charlotte Peacock, and Erlend Clouston for your kind assistance and interest. The website which accompanies the book was created by Neil Hedley of Hedley Enterprises, who was a joy to work with, and who also appreciates a good coffee. Thanks also go to the contributors; Crawford Paris, Karla Hall, Shayne MacFaull, Cheryl Roberts, Lucy MacDonald and Tony Yule.

With thanks to my mum, dad and family, and to G and J - for all your love, support and help.

This book is dedicated to Charlie, my dearest of Deeside Way companions, always.

ABOUT THE AUTHOR

Kelly Morrison is a writer and heritage enthusiast – passionate about conserving natural, cultural and built heritage through connecting people and places. A local of Aberdeen and Deeside, having lived most of her life along various sections of the Deeside Way, she loves the simple joys of walking, exploring the beauty of nature, and good coffee.

Kelly has an MA in Heritage and Interpretation and currently works in academia on a digital heritage storytelling project. She has previously worked in regional economic development and placemaking, as well as for the National Trust for Scotland, and she is a board member of the North East Scotland Preservation Trust.

www.kellymorrison.co.uk

REFERENCES

1. Shepherd, N. (2019). *The Colours of Deeside*. In C. Peacock (Ed.), *Wild Geese (p.48)*. Galileo Publishers.

2. Shepherd, N. (2011). *The Living Mountain (p.108)*. Canongate Books.

3. Jamieson, D. and Wilson, W.S. (2001). *Old Royal Deeside (p.3)*. Stenlake Publishing Ltd.

4. Wyness, F. (1968) *Royal Valley The Story of the Aberdeenshire Dee (p.2.)*. Alex. P. Reid Son

5. Brown, I. (1952). *Summer in Scotland (p.156)*. Collins.

6. Jamieson, D. and Wilson, W.S. (2001). *Old Royal Deeside (p.3)*. Stenlake Publishing Ltd.

7. Shepherd, N. (2011). *The Living Mountain (pp.22-23)*. Canongate Books.

8. Jamieson, D. and Wilson, W.S. (2001). *Old Royal Deeside (p.3)*. Stenlake Publishing Ltd.

9. Jamieson, D. and Wilson, W.S. (2001). *Old Royal Deeside (p.3)*. Stenlake Publishing Ltd.

10. Deeside Way (n.d.). *Deeside Way*. Retrieved from **http://www.deesideway.org/**

11. Sustrans (n.d.). *National Cycle Network routes in North and North East Scotland*. Retrieved from **https://www.sustrans.org.uk/find-a-route-on-the-national-cycle-network/national-cycle-network-routes-in-north-and-north-east-scotland/**

12. Historic Environment Scotland (1990). *Guild Street Aberdeen Railway Station and road overbridge*. Retrieved from **http://portal.historicenvironment.scot/designation/LB20673?msclkid=aa81964cd16511ec84d24ef3b592c716**

13. Jamieson, D. and Wilson, W.S. (2003). *Old Lower Deeside (p.7)*. Stenlake Publishing Ltd.

14. The Silver City Vault (n.d.). *Interior of the David Welch Winter Gardens*. Retrieved from **https://www.silvercityvault.org.uk/index.php?a=QuickSearch&q=david%20welch&WINID=1666030856916**

15. Aberdeen City Council (n.d.). *Old Deeside Line: Duthie Park [Interpretation board]* N.p: Aberdeen City Council.

16. Aberdeen City Council (n.d.). *Old Deeside Line: Holburn Station [Interpretation board]* N.p: Aberdeen City Council.

17. Grace's Guide to British Industrial Heritage (n.d). *James Abernethy and Co*. Retrieved from **https://www.gracesguide.co.uk/James_Abernethy_and_Co**

18. Garthdee Allotments (2018). *IYN – What a result!* Retrieved from **https://garthdeeallotments.org/iyn-what-a-result/**

19. Aberdeen City Council (n.d.). *Old Deeside Line: Pitfodels Station [Interpretation board]* N.p: Aberdeen City Council.

20. Andonova, D. (2021, November 9). *Has Banksy come to visit?* The Press and Journal, p.3.

21. Aberdeen City Council (n.d.). *Old Deeside Line: Cults Station [Interpretation board]* N.p: Aberdeen City Council.

22. Aberdeen City Council (n.d.). *Old Deeside Line: West Cults [Interpretation board]* N.p: Aberdeen City Council.

23. Andrews, K. (2021) Wanderers: *A History of Women Walking (pp. 187-188)*. Reaktion Books Ltd.

24. Aberdeen City Council (n.d.). *Old Deeside Line: Bieldside Station [Interpretation board]* N.p: Aberdeen City Council.

25. Jackson, D. (1994) *The Deeside Line: The North-East's Royal Railway (p.14)*. Great North of Scotland Railway Association.

26. Jamieson, D. and Wilson, W.S. (2003). *Old Lower Deeside (p.22)*. Stenlake Publishing Ltd.

27. Aberdeen City Council (n.d.). *Old Deeside Line: Culter Station [Interpretation board]* N.p: Aberdeen City Council.

28. Culter Community Council (2007). *Culter Explorer [Leaflet]* Aberdeen: Thistle Reprographics.

29. National Trust for Scotland. (n.d.). *Drum Castle, Garden & Estate*. Retrieved from **https://www.nts.org.uk/visit/places/drum-castle**

30. Maxtone, G. and Cooper, M. (2018). *Then and Now on the Great North (p.20)*. Great North of Scotland Railway Association.

31. Coutts, J. (1899) *Dictionary of Deeside (p.254)*. Aberdeen – The University Press.

32. Shepherd, N. (2019). *The Colours of Deeside*. In C. Peacock (Ed.), *Wild Geese (p.48)*. Galileo Publishers.

33. Maxtone, G. and Cooper, M. (2018). *Then and Now on the Great North (p.22)*. Great North of Scotland RailwayAssociation.

34. Jackson, D. (2008) *Royal Deeside's Railway (p.13)*. Great North of Scotland Railway Association.

35. BBC News (2013) *World's Oldest Calendar Discovered in Scottish Field [Online]*. Available from: https://www.bbc.co.uk/news/uk-scotland-north-east-orkney-shetland-23286928 [Accessed: 15 July 2022]

36. National Trust for Scotland. (n.d.). *Crathes Castle, Garden & Estate*. Retrieved from https://www.nts.org.uk/visit/places/drum-castle

37. BBC News (2021) *Hundreds of prehistoric tools found along river [Online]*. Available from https://www.bbc.co.uk/news/articles/cz88vzkdgyeo [Accessed: 09 July 2022]

38. Kagge, E. (2018) *Walking: One Step at a Time (p.17)*. Viking, an imprint of Penguin Random House.

39. Deeside Way (n.d.). *Deeside Way – Banchory to Aboyne*. Retrieved from http://www.deesideway.org/walks/banchory-to-aboyne/

40. Shepherd, N. (2019). *The Colours of Deeside*. In C. Peacock (Ed.), *Wild Geese (p.45)*. Galileo Publishers.

41. Jamieson, D. and Wilson, W.S. (2001). *Old Royal Deeside .17)*. Stenlake Publishing Ltd.

42. K.A.D.E.T (1993) *Kincardine O'Neil [Interpretation board]* N.p.

43. K.A.D.E.T (1993) *Kincardine O'Neil [Interpretation board]* N.p.

44. Kincardine O'Neil Community Association (2016). *Walks around Kincardine O'Neil [Booklet]* Aberdeen: Thistle Reprographics

45. Kincardine O'Neil Community Association (2016). *Walks around Kincardine O'Neil: Short Walks [Booklet]* Aberdeen: Thistle Reprographics.

46. Kincardine O'Neil Community Association (2016). *Walks around Kincardine O'Neil: Short Walks [Booklet]* Aberdeen: Thistle Reprographics.

47. Marr, G.J. (2014) *The Old Deeside Road Revisited (p.13)*. Deeside Books.

48. Smith, R. (1989) *Valley of the Dee (p.23)*. Aberdeen University Library.

49. Jamieson, D. and Wilson, W.S. (2001). *Old Royal Deeside (p.24)*. Stenlake Publishing Ltd.

50. Geddes, J. (2001) *Deeside and the Mearns: an illustrated architectural guide (p.117)* The Rutland Press.

51. NatureScot (n.d.) *Muir of Dinnet: Crannog Island [Interpretation board]* N.p: NatureScot.

52. NatureScot (n.d.). *Muir of Dinnet: Castle Island [Interpretation board]* N.p: NatureScot.

53. NatureScot (n.d.). *Muir of Dinnet: National Nature Reserve [Leaflet]* N.p: NatureScot.

54. Smith, R. (1989) *Valley of the Dee (p.37)*. Aberdeen University Library.

55. Canmore (n.d.). *Meikle Kinord*. Retrieved from https://canmore.org.uk/site/33986/meikle-kinord

56. Johnston, J. (1934). *Place-Names of Scotland (p.123)*. John Murray Edition.

57. Jamieson, D. and Wilson, W.S. (2001). *Old Royal Deeside (p.40)*. Stenlake Publishing Ltd.

58. History with Boots On (n.d.). *The Needle [Interpretation marker]* N.p: History with Boots On.

59. Coutts, J. (1899) *Dictionary of Deeside (p.3)*. Aberdeen – The University Press.

60. Jamieson, D. and Wilson, W.S. (2001). *Old Royal Deeside (p.3)*. Stenlake Publishing Ltd.

61. Smith, R. (1994). *25 Walks Deeside (p.42)*. HMSO.

62. Smith, R. (1994). *25 Walks Deeside (p.43)*. HMSO.

63. The RIBA Journal (2020) *Ace caff with Moxon Architects; very nice studio attached [online]*. Available from: https://www.ribaj.com/buildings/quarry-studios-crathie-aberdeenshire-moxon-architects-tamarchan-cafe [Accessed 15 June 2022]

64. Jamieson, D. and Wilson, W.S. (2001). *Old Royal Deeside (p.3)*. Stenlake Publishing Ltd.

65. Jamieson, D. and Wilson, W.S. (2001). *Old Royal Deeside (p.49)*. Stenlake Publishing Ltd.

66. Jamieson, D. and Wilson, W.S. (2001). *Old Royal Deeside (p.45)*. Stenlake Publishing Ltd.

67. Shepherd, N. (2011). *The Living Mountain (p.1)*. Canongate Books.

68. Wyness, F. (1968) *Royal Valley – The Story of the Aberdeenshire Dee (p.291.)*. Alex. P. Reid Son

INDEX

ADDITIONAL WALKS

MUIR OF DINNET NATIONAL NATURE RESERVE

did you spot any of these on the route?

NATURE ON THE DEESIDE WAY

- ☐ Kestrel
- ☐ Owl
- ☐ Red Deer
- ☐ Beech Tree
- ☐ Alpaca
- ☐ Horse
- ☐ Rabbit
- ☐ Larch Tree
- ☐ Grouse
- ☐ Pheasant
- ☐ Buzzard
- ☐ Mushroom
- ☐ Wild Garlic

- ☐ Shetland Pony
- ☐ Swan
- ☐ Butterfly
- ☐ Red Squirrel
- ☐ Roe Deer
- ☐ Hare
- ☐ Sheep
- ☐ Waxwing
- ☐ Fox
- ☐ Lapwing
- ☐ Oak Tree
- ☐ Robin
- ☐ Pigs

First Edition. Published 2022.

Text copyright © Kelly Morrison, 2022

Front Cover & Photo of Author: Elin Beattie

All photos: © Kelly Morrison, © Elin Beattie*, © Charlene Cheesman** except:

Photos courtesy of, with much thanks: **Estate of Nan Shepherd** p43(2); **Aberdeen City Libraries/ The Silver City Vault** p24, p37(2), **Crawford Paris** p39, 186, 187; **Shayne MacFaull** p88(2). **Hidden Scotland** p83, 84, 85(3); **ARRA Textiles** p 110(2); **eguide Scotland** p124, 125(2); **Tarmachan Cafe** p165, 166 (2); **The Highlanders Bakehouse** p168(2); **Dawn Carnegie** p169; **Martin Bennie** via Unsplash p183. *(reproduced with permissions)*

*Photos by Elin Beattie: p5, 8, 11, 26, 36(2), 40, 51, 62, 63, 71(2), 76, 92, 94, 95, 105, 112, 114(2), 122(2), 123(2), 128, 129, 132, 155, 156, 163, 174, 176, 177, 179, 180, 182.

**Photos by Charlene Cheesman: p15, 16, 18, 21(2), 25(3), 61. 82(3), 82, 87(2), 91(2), 109(1), 138(1), 143, 150

All rights reserved. No part of this publication may be reproduced or transmitted in any form or by any means, in part or in whole for any use, in any form or any means without prior permission in writing from the author.

References are complied to the best of the author's ability and knowledge.

Disclaimer

All rights reserved. All text and images are exclusive to Kelly Morrison unless otherwise stated and credited, and may not be reproduced or transmitted in any form or by any means, in part or in full for any use without prior written permission.

The locations and walks in this book have been researched, visited and tested by the author herself and are believed to be true at the time of publishing in December 2022. The author can accept no responsibility for any unforeseen circumstances encountered while using this companion book or following the suggested routes. Readers should be aware of their own skill level and experience, as well as those of their group.

the
deeside
way

TO CRATHIE & BRAEMAR
BALLATER
MORVEN
• TULLICH
• CAMBUS O'MAY
LOCH KINORD
MOUNT KEEN
• DINNET
• ABOYNE
CRAIGLICH
• KINCARDINE O'NEIL
CLACHNABEN
• POTARCH
SCOLTY
• BANCHORY
MEIKLE TAP
CRATHES •
• DRUMOAK
• CULTER
• CULTS
ABERDEEN

W
N
S
E